CONCILIUM

concilium

1995/1

THE BIBLE AS CULTURAL HERITAGE

Edited by

Wim Beuken and Sean Freyne

SCM Press · London
Orbis Books · Maryknoll

Published by SCM Press Ltd, 26–30 Tottenham Road, London N1
and by Orbis Books, Maryknoll, NY 10545

ISBN: 0 334 03030 7 (UK)
ISBN: 0 88344 882 3 (USA)

Typeset at The Spartan Press Ltd, Lymington, Hants
Printed by Mackays of Chatham, Kent

Concilium: Published February, April, June, August, October, December.

Contents

Editorial   The Bible as Cultural Heritage
  WIM BEUKEN AND SEAN FREYNE   vii

I · From World to Scroll: The Bible and Its Cultures   1

'From the Midst of the Nations': The Bible as a Gateway
to Ancient Near Eastern Cultures   3
  OTHMAR KEEL

Jews and Greeks: The Diaspora as an Experience of
Cultural Diversification   14
  JACQUES VAN RUITEN

'Telling in Their Own Tongues': Old and Modern
Bible Translations as Expressions of Ethnic Cultural Identity   24
  WILLARD G. OXTOBY

'Neither Jew nor Greek': The Challenge of Building
One Multicultural Religious Community   36
  JOHN K. RICHES

II · From Scroll to World: The Bible and the Making of
Culture   45

The Bible in Arts and Literature: Source of Inspiration for
Poets and Painters   47
  DAVID JASPER

The Bible and the Discovery of the World: Mission,
Colonization and Foreign Development   61
  ARNULF CAMPS

III · From Scroll to Book of Life: The Bible as
Source of Human Values   71

New Ways of Reading the Bible in the Cultural Settings
of the New World   73
    JEAN-PIERRE RUIZ

The Bible as Magna Carta of Movements for Liberation
and Human Rights   85
    GEORGE M. SOARES-PRABHU

The Bible and the Preservation of the World   97
    NORMAN SOLOMON

'Behold I Make All Things New': The Final Statement
of the Fourth Plenary Assembly of the Catholic Biblical
Federation   108
    TERESA OKURE

Special Column   121

Contributors   125

Editorial

The Bible as Cultural Heritage

Concilium has always sought to honour the statement of the Second Vatican Council that the Bible should be the heart of theology. Not merely has there been a regular number of the journal devoted to exegesis (latterly in conjunction with church history), but other numbers also have invariably contained a scriptural article on the topic being explored. Over past years the link with church history has posed a new kind of challenge for the editors in seeking to give the number a more coherent focus. This has been achieved, on the whole successfully, we believe, by attending to the ways in which a biblical theme – Exodus, Truth, Messiah – has been received and developed within the post-biblical tradition also. Inevitably, this has meant a rather restricted view of church history, and so it has been decided that this particular experiment should be discontinued. After this present number *Concilium* will revert to having a separate number of exegesis alone.

It seems appropriate, therefore, that the present number, *The Bible as Cultural Heritage*, should act as a kind of companion volume to a previous number, *The Bible and its Readers* (1991/1). In that issue the focus was on reading from a theological perspective – the ways in which the Bible has been read in different ecclesial and religious situations throughout the centuries. The Bible, containing the Old and New Testaments – *ho Biblos* 'the Book' – is a creation of Christian faith. Representing the church's own distillation of its received inheritance of authoritative writings from earlier centuries, including the Hebrew Scriptures in their Greek translation, the Septuagint (LXX). The tendency was to seek a theological unity for this diverse collection from both Testaments, in terms either of a christological centre (e.g. Justin Martyr) or divinely inspired authorship (*theopneustos*, II Tim.3.16). The sixteenth-century Reformation, with its critique of what its authors saw as the corrupting influence of tradition, made the

Bible as a single book the focus of its reform, a perspective that was highlighted by Luther's classic translation, which was to play a very significant part in the success of the Reformation in German-speaking lands, as well as contributing to the development of the German language itself. Of course it had its forerunner in St Jerome's fifth-century translation into Latin, the Vulgate, which had also made a powerful contribution to Western Christendom. Luther's translation was to be the precursor of further translations into vernacular languages, most notably, perhaps, the King James Version into English, published in 1611, and the Staten Version into Dutch, published in 1637, which are still regarded as classics.

These translations into modern languages, the direct result of the Reformer's sole scripture principle, were intended to make the Bible immediate and accessible to the people as a religious document, yet paradoxically the overall effect was to contribute towards making it a collection from the remote past. This gave rise to its study as a collection written in ancient languages and in need of having the original text established. The seventeenth-century Enlightenment with its focus on human reason and Deistic beliefs was to erode further the authority of the Bible as offering a coherent and acceptable world-view in the light of scientific discoveries and the rational critique of religion. The nineteenth-century romantic revival and the liberal attempt to retrieve the essence of the biblical message could not of themselves restore the Bible to its erstwhile pre-eminence as *the Book*. The separation between faith and reason, history and revelation, that had occurred made such a nostalgic return to the mediaeval world view impossible. Yet for all that, the Bible has continued to nourish the spiritual lives of endless millions, has been translated into countless languages and continues to be the world's 'Best Seller'.

It is against the backdrop of this brief and potted sketch of the Bible's history of reception that this issue of *Concilium* was planned. The very expression 'cultural heritage', clumsy though it may be, seeks to highlight the Bible as something precious, not just in religious terms, but from a broader perspective also. Such a distinction between religion and culture is a modern one that would have been unthinkable in previous ages when all of human culture was perceived as religious, that is, directly controlled and guided by divine agency. In our post-enlightenment world we have come, even as believers, to accept that the various human sciences and disciplines can legitimately interpret the world from their own, secular perspectives. This has in turn led to the recognition that the great religious traditions, including the Jewish and Christian ones, of which their sacred literatures are a reflection, have, despite the ambiguities that are inherent in all human enterprises, contributed enormously towards the development of human life in the world. One can think of the areas of language, law, literature, representational art, geographical exploration and the human and natural sciences as the most obvious and important examples. This issue is interested in exploring this broader aspect of the Bible's contribution to Western, indeed to global civilization. It will emerge that the contribution has been hugely significant, even when limitations of space and time have made it impossible to cover every aspect that one might have wished.

It quickly became apparent that the Bible was capable of making such a 'secular' contribution to human civilization, and continues to do so, because it is itself the product of its own variegated cultural environment, from second-millennium BCE Mesopotamia and Egypt through ninth-century BCE Israel to first-century Greece and Rome. As such it is the mirror of several ancient civilizations whose achievements lie at the root of our own contemporary world and on whose visions we have built. The discovery and study of artefacts and documents from these ancient cultures is the direct result of the Bible's continued attraction in the modern world. Without the stimulus of seeking to understand this ancient collection of writings with its continuing relevance for life, it is doubtful if we would be as informed about the history of human civilization as we are. In this regard we can make our own the saying that was current in the early Middle Ages as people began to rediscover the glories of the classical past that had been lost in the so-called Dark Ages: 'We today are like dwarfs, carried along on the shoulders of the giants of the past; we can see farther because we have been raised higher.' As a window on the past, the Bible reflects several axial periods of human history and challenges us to consider how our own age and century may be viewed in respect of lasting human achievement from the perspective of a millenium hence.

Even as it reflects the cultures which produced it, the Bible also has had the capacity to shape cultures based on its stories, its imagery, its legal traditions, its view of the world . . . in many different settings and periods. These aspects are widely acknowledged and easily discerned today, even by those who would claim to have long abandoned its strictly religious message in our secular age. The task today is not to reify the text through a slavish adherence to the letter, the perennial temptation for all varieties of fundamentalisms. Nor is it correct to retreat to a form of 'archaeologism', fascinating though it undoubtedly is to study the ancient worlds behind the text for their own sakes. The failure of such an approach is the Romantic attachment to the past as though it represented some golden age of innocence, thereby avoiding the challenges of the present. The safest way to ensure that our heritage becomes a genuine inheritance for others after us is to continue to struggle with and for the basic insights of the Bible with regard to the meaning and dignity of human life in this world, irrespective of whether one's perspective is 'religious' or 'secular'. These different aspects of our topic are reflected in different ways in the three sections that comprise this number of *Concilium*. It is the hope of the editors that a correct balance has been achieved in terms of the past, present and future aspects of our topic and the challenges with which it confronts us as we continue the search for peace, justice and the integrity of creation, the core message with which the Bible presents us in its many and varied accents.

Wim Beuken
Sean Freyne

Note
The editors had planned an article on 'The Bible and the Structures of Western Society'. They regret not having been able to provide a good article about this subject-matter on time.

I · From World to Scroll: The Bible and Its Cultures

'From the Midst of the Nations': The Bible as a Gateway to Ancient Near Eastern Cultures

Othmar Keel

Is it not contrary to the real intention of biblical books to regard them as a gateway through which cultural values or earlier 'pagan' cultures have come down to us and to read the Bible itself as the expression of a culture?

1. The Bible as the expression of a culture?

If one has grown up with exegetical literature which asked about the *kergyma* of the Deuteronomist, the *kergyma* of the Priestly writing or the (theological) 'aim' of each chapter of the Old Testament (as does the *Biblischer Kommentar*), the suggestion that the Bible should be read as cultural material might seem a profanation.

Compared with their colleagues in the middle of the twentieth century CE, some Jews of the second century BCE like the grandson of Jesus Sirach or the author of II Maccabees are less theocentric. Their remarks are of special interest, because in their prefaces they are the first biblical writers to make explicit statements about the aims they are pursuing in their books. At all events they do not see just one cause for writing, so that one could assign one kergyma to a work and one 'aim' to a section. For example, in his preface the grandson of Jesus Sirach, who translated his grandfather's work into Greek, describes the content of the 'law, prophets and other writings' very vaguely as 'many' and 'great' and the result of occupation with them as 'instruction and wisdom' (*paideia* and *sophia*), terms which one is as justified in connecting with culture as with a particular theology. The aim of his grandfather's work, like his own, is a way of life grounded in the Law which could be denoted with the modern term 'Jewish way of life'.

In view of the positions adopted by dialectical theology, it seems almost frivolous when the redactor of II Maccabees states as the first of the various aims of his work 'entertainment and pleasure' (*psychagogia*, 2.25), an aim which is surprising, given the zealots and martyrs who are the heroes of this book.

If the scope of individual biblical books can hardly be grasped appropriately with such vague cultural aims, on the other hand it has to be emphasized that an attempt to construct the kerygma e.g. of the Song of Songs hardly represents an adequate approach to it.

2. Religious norm versus culture

The character of the Bible as religious teaching and obligation which rabbis and church fathers postulated in the first centuries after Christ made it impossible to perceive it and develop it further as cultural material, and gave it a one-sidedly religious normative character. A culture cannot limit itself to discovering and putting into effect the secrets and the expressed wills of its deity/ies, but must cover and shape all aspects of human life. That was also the case in ancient Israel.

The consequences of the 'personality change' in the biblical library at the beginning of our era are particularly vivid in the case of the Song of Songs. A rabbinic tradition illuminates this in a touching way when it makes Johanan ben Nuri (c. 110 CE) pronounce: 'Anyone who quotes a verse from the Song of Songs and uses it as a kind of (profane) song, or anyone who quotes any verse of scripture inappropriately in a wedding house (or at a feast) brings disaster upon the world. For the Torah (the whole scripture as revelation) dressed itself in garments of mourning, appeared before God, and said before him: "Lord of the world, your children have made me a kind of zither on which the pagans play!" Then God said to her: "My daughter, with what should they then occupy themselves when they eat and drink?" She replied: "If they are expert in scripture, they may occupy themselves with the law, the prophets and writings; if they are expert in the tradition they may occupy themselves with the Mishnah, the Halakhah and the Aggadah; if they are experts in the Talmud, they may occupy themselves at Passover with the regulations for Passover, at the Feast of Weeks with the regulations for the Feast of Weeks, at Tabernacles with the regulations for the Feast of Tabernacles"' (Sanhedrin 101a, Baraita). Those who handed this down presumably supposed that God is content with this answer. But is God? Can God be content with this proposal of the Torah when in the beginning God said in the Garden that it was not good for man to remain alone (with God) (Gen.2.18).

But for the moment, with the help of typology and allegory, the limitation of scripture to revelation established itself for around 1500 years, even in the case of the Song of Songs.

3. Back to culture

First the Renaissance, then humanism, the Enlightenment and Romanticism have restored its human aspect to scripture, bit by bit. Here above all G. E. Lessing and J. G. Herder put forward the view that the old Testament contained testimonies from the childhood days of the human race, products of a still childlike spirit or, in theological terms, divine measures for the education of the human race.

However, the notion of Hebrew humanism as the earliest written attestation of human culture (theologically often understood as the purest transmitted form of the primal revelation) was soon massively put in question by the activity of researchers and explorers in the nineteenth century. The effort to get to know and describe the habits and customs of as many peoples and tribes as possible also embraced past cultures. Thus between 1837 and 1841 there appeared J. G. Wilkinson's six-volume work *Manners and Customs of the Ancient Egyptians ... Derived from a Comparison of the ... Monuments still Existing with the Accounts of Ancient Authors*. A. H. Layard did the same thing for the Assyrians. However, their monuments were no longer accessible and first had to be excavated. The second part of Layard's famous 1849 account of his activity in this direction, *Nineveh and its Remains*, similarly contains 'An Enquiry into the Manners and Arts of the Ancient Assyrians'. Soon it became clear that not only Egyptian but also Mesopotamian culture was considerably older than that of the Bible.

This greater age did not just relate to the material aspects. In 1874 C. W. Goodwin pointed out that the poems of the Song of Songs had parallels in earlier Egyptian love poetry. G. Smith's 1876 *Chaldean Account of Genesis* made known Babylonian forerunners to the biblical narratives of the creation and especially the flood. In winter 1901/2 French archaeologists discovered a stele with the legal corpus of the Babylonian king Hammurabi (18th century BCE), in which there were numerous legal clauses corresponding almost word for word to what, according to the biblical tradition, is said to have been revealed to Moses on Sinai. In 1910 A. Weigal published the first monograph on Akenaten and celebrated him as the founder of a pure belief in God and as a forerunner of Christ. In 1924 the German Egyptologist A. Erman demonstrated that Proverbs 22.17–23.11 draws heavily on the ancient Egyptian teaching of Amenemope. In his 1929 commentary on the Psalms, H. Gunkel discovered the close connection between the picture of the king in the so-called messianic psalms and Egyptian notions of the king. This robbed the Psalms of their supposedly prophetic character. The unique hymn to creation, Psalm 104, is partially dependent on Egyptian hymns to the sun. The discovery of the Ugaritic texts has shown that the powerful Psalm 29 is an adaptation of a hymn to Baal. More and more letters from Mari on the Middle Euphrates, the home of Balaam, bear witness to lively prophetic activity long before the biblical prophets. Deuteronomy has its model as a treaty in neo-Assyrian vassal treaties. In addition, there is the influence of ancient Near Eastern pictorial art on the Israelite world of ideas (cherubim, seraphim, Lord of the animals in Job 39, the king in triumph, and so on). There no longer seems to be a biblical book or theme for which parallels or forerunners have not been mentioned from the ancient Near East or ancient Egypt.

Israel received impulses and stimuli from every direction. The effort to derive the forms of speech, similes and metaphors of the Song of Songs exclusively from Egypt (G. Gerleman) has proved just as much of a failure as the attempt to understand them all in terms of the Near East (M. Pope). Care must be taken with each individual poem to see whether it is autochtonous or whether it can only be interpreted in the light of Egyptian or Ancient Near Eastern traditions (O. Keel); here in turn distinctions must be made between Hittite, Aramaic, Assyrian, Bablylonian and Persian influence, and so on.

4. Culture versus revelation

The theological construct of a primal revelation with which people attempted to cope with this new information quickly fell in on itself when scientists discovered just what gigantic periods of time had elapsed since the first appearance of human beings and how much biblical notions and formulations had in common with those of the great ancient neighbouring cultures, whether of Egypt or the Near East, but not with those of India, China or Latin America.

The challenge which the discoveries of the nineteenth and early twentieth centuries posed to a more or less decided belief in revelation were focused dramatically in the Babel-Bibel dispute. It was sparked off by a lantern show by the Assyriologist F. Delitzsch, which he gave in Berlin on

13 January 1902 in the presence of Kaiser Wilhelm II. The lecture produced virtually nothing that was not already familiar to those in the know. But thanks to the Kaiser's presence it was given the greatest publicity, and thus reached a broad public, still firmly believing in revelation, which was completely unprepared for Delitzsch's concentrated load of information. Deeply hurt, this public accused Delitzsch of denying revelation, stoned the messenger, and thus believed that it had defused his message.

Those with more insight, like Gunkel in his 1895 work *Creation and Chaos*, had pointed out even before the Babel-Bibel dispute that the question was not *whether* old material had been worked over in the Bible but *how* it had been worked over. It was here that the special character of the Bible and its theological significance were to be found. However, this criterion for making a distinction seemed too gradual and too slight to the dialectical theology of the 1920s and 1930s, for example that of Karl Barth. Asserting that the Bible is about revelation and faith, and that the ancient Near Eastern cultures are only about myth and religion, this theology caused a split which could not be bridged, yet which the subject-matter could not justify.

From the 1960s onwards, exegesis returned increasingly strongly to the questions of Gunkel and his colleagues.

5. The Bible – a gateway to the cultures of the ancient Near East?

In surface area, ancient Israel was a tiny country. The heartland of Judah comprised about 3000 square kilometres, and at their greatest extent Israel and Judah were not very much bigger than the small state of Lebanon. At most only parts of the coastal region, densely populated today, were part of it. In the south at all times the coast was in the hands of the Philistines, and in the north in the hands of the Phoenicians.

As part of the land bridge between Africa and the Near East, Israel, while standing somewhat apart from the great international trade routes, was in contact not only with its immediate neighbours but also with the ancient political and cultural great powers in Egypt and Mesopotamia, though it was mostly more a kind of developing country than a partner of equal status. Israelites and Judahites, men and women, emigrated to Egypt or were deported to Babylon without losing contact with their homeland. Foreign traders and soldiers went through the country. Between around 1500 and 1150 the whole country had been an Egyptian colony. After Israel became a state, a number of Pharaohs attempted to restore the old supremacy. The Assyrians ruled from c. 730–630. After a short pause their legacy was taken over by the Babylonians, who in 539 were replaced by the Persians, until in 333 BCE these had to yield to Alexander and his successors.

Judah and Jerusalem were not only small, but also took their place among the nations at a late stage (Ezek. 5.5). Whereas Lessing and Herder saw the Bible as a collection of poems from the infancy of the human race, we now know that its texts, composed between 1050 and 50 BCE, form a relatively late corpus in the framework of the ancient Near East. Sumerian literature begins about 2600 BCE in Fara (Shuruppag) with temple hymns, myths, and didactic narrative literature. The earliest religious literature of the Egyptians, the so-called Pyramid Texts, were preserved for the first time in writing in the Pyramid of Una (c. 2350 BCE). The Bible is roughly as far distant from these earliest works of literature known to us as it is from the present. Despite some attempts (on evidence which is either bad or non-existent) to derive the bulk of the biblical texts (on the basis of the latest stages of redaction) from the Persian or even the Hellenistic period, the majority of the biblical texts are to be dated to the pre-Hellenistic period, and are to be seen as a late product of the cultural sphere of the ancient Near East and ancient Egypt.

Given the geographical and historical facts sketched out above, the question arises whether Israel did not lack the critical mass to produce a special, original and largely brilliant culture of its own, and whether the biblical writings, like the pictorial art of ancient Israel, did not consist mainly of imports and local adaptations of Egyptian, Aramaic, Assyrian and Babylonian creations. That is not just a conjecture deduced from geographical and historical facts, but over wide areas is substantiated by the examples in section 3 above and similar observations.

However, in contrast to the palace archive of Nineveh and the temple libraries of Egypt, the ancient Near Eastern texts taken over by the Israelites were not buried (or even destroyed) and only rediscovered in the nineteenth and twentieth centuries, but handed down without interruption and disseminated throughout the world in countless translations. This tremendous work of popularization has transferred many motifs from the ancient Near East into countless cultural memories (pictorial art, literature), with the result that for example the interpretation of Mesopotamian cities and temple towers is *down to the present day* more markedly influenced by the story of the 'tower of Babel' (Gen. 11) than by the scholarly work on the Mesopotamian ziggurats of whole generations of Near Eastern archaeologists.

6. Or a collection of caricatures?

But in view of the story of the tower of Babel the question also arises whether the Old Testament has not produced polemical caricatures and satires of ancient Near Eastern phenomena rather than understanding and benevolent mediations. It is not difficult to see, and is generally recognized, that the depictions of the cults of foreign deities, from Dagon among the Philistines to Marduk in Babylon, are mocking caricatures. As a rule the biblical tradition commandeered hymns, myths and other texts about foreign deities and claimed them for its God (see section 3 above), or caricatured things by deliberately or unintentionally misunderstanding them and making those who worshipped images worshippers of 'wood and stone'.

Just as we find a powerful anti-Judaism in individual texts of the New Testament, so in Old Testament texts we find a deliberate 'anti-Canaanism'. Researches in the last two decades have shown that Israel is largely to be understood as part of the autochthonous population of the land, and the polemic against the nations which were in the land before Israel may initially have been a wide-ranging polemic within Israel. Deuteronomic and Deuteronomistic texts in particular set apart the religion and ethics of the peoples 'who lived in the land before Israel', artificially and with every means of Israelite polemic. In the wake of this polemic, for example even today the 'Canaanite' Baal demanding bloody human sacrifices is contrasted with the God of Israel and his friendly concern for human beings. But despite Deut. 12.31, there is not a single piece of evidence for 'Canaanite' human sacrifices from the second millennium BCE. In the first millennium very different Near Eastern cultures, including that of Judah, seem to have toyed with ideas of human sacrifice, among others Israel (Gen. 22). The charge of human sacrifice made against the pre-Israelite inhabitants of the land is as unfounded as the charge of child sacrifice later made against early Christianity or mediaeval Judaism.

There is similar polemic in the sexual sphere. Leviticus 18.6–23 lists a series of specific sexual tabus which held in the extended Israelite family. The secondary framework in Leviticus 18.1–5 and 24–30 claims that Egyptians and Canaanites above all offended against these tabus. Thus at a stroke Canaanite men and women, Egyptian men and women, were discriminated against for certain sexual practices. The story of Judah and Tamar in Genesis 38 unmasks this attitude as Judahite and male hypocrisy. But later the charge of sexual perversion becomes a standard element of the polemic against the 'Canaanites', rejected by God, and is no longer investigated.

The anxious, violent and polemical dissociation from the 'Canaanites' led to the loss of much sensitivity and delight in the 'natural'. Whereas the stories of the patriarchs still have them planting trees in holy places (Gen. 21.33), and in early post-exilic period trees in the temple sphere bore witness to the power of God's blessing (Pss. 52.10; 92.13f.), according to Hecataeus of Abdera they were all cut down in the Persian period to exclude any suspicion of the cultic worship of 'wood and stone' (Josephus, *Contra Apionem* I, 199).

7. Positive reception

But the Old Testament did not just commandeer ancient Near Eastern cultural material as an element of its own symbol-system or hand it down in a polemical distortion. We often find critical and distorted accounts in the Hebrew Bible side by side with admiring accounts of the same theme. Thus the prophetic Exodus tradition, influenced by prophecy, sketches a very critical picture of the political culture of Egypt, while the Joseph story, stamped by wisdom, presents it as having in part been shaped by a Hebrew and thus as acceptable, even exemplary.

Similarly, the position of the prophets on beauty, adornment, cosmetics and eroticism is diametrically opposed to that of the Song of Songs. How remote the Song of Songs is from a narrow Yahwism which tolerates only an oath by the God of Israel (Jer. 5.7; 12.16) is shown by the often-repeated oath by the gazelles and hinds of the wilderness (Song of Songs 2.7; 3.5). The shy, agile beasts belong in the sphere of the goddess of love. An oath by them is just a weakly disguised oath by her.

The tradition of synagogue and church clearly detected in the Song of Songs the presence of typically 'Canaanite' values which it slandered. For centuries its 'personality' had to be changed by typologizing and allegorical interpretation to make it acceptable to synagogue and church. People like Theodore of Mopsuestia (fourth/fifth centuries) or Sebastian Castellio (sixteenth century), to whom this alteration seemed intellectually dishonest, and who argued for a literal understanding, drew the conclusion from this that the book should be removed from the canon.

It was a break with a tradition extending over almost two thousand years when, following *Divino afflante Spiritu* (1943), some Dominicans (M. A. van den Oudenrijn, A. M. Dubarle, and J. P. Audet) in the early 1950s established a literal understanding of the Song of Songs in the Catholic church as well, and thus *de facto* introduced a rehabilitation of Canaanite values which had been discriminated against over millennia. These efforts have been given powerful support over the last two decades from feminist theology. The injustices of the adolescent polemical efforts of Israel to detach itself from its 'Canaanite' parents (cf. Ezek. 16.3) can thus finally be recognized and as far as possible be made good. They can join forces with the similar attempt to unmask and demolish the anti-Judaism which early Christianity developed in the New Testament, in search of its own identity, and rediscover the quite authentic and genuine values of Judaism.

8. Some contributions

Something essential would be missing were we to treat the topic of 'the Old Testament and the cultures of the ancient Near East' only under the headings of admiration (Joseph story), tacit adoption (Song of Songs), commandeering (section 3), demarcations and polemical distortions. What was the catalyst which led to one or other reaction, and can one describe this catalyst as the distinctive and specific characteristic of the culture of Israel and Judah? The question sounds like the question about the centre, the basic message, the basic impulse of the Old Testament. The discovery that different texts in the Old Testament react in very different ways to the same cultural entities (particular forms of eroticism, politics) makes us mistrustful of the assumption that such a centre can be constructed.

To be specific, though originally Yahweh was probably also shared with the Midianites (Ex. 18), the bond of Israel is to Yahweh and his territory. But that does not mean much. Yahweh is a proper name. It is not very significant whether a people worships the storm god under the name Teshub, Hadad, Baal or another name. And it was nothing special in the first half of the first millennium BCE for a god to have his people. The Assyrians had Assur, the Ammonites Milkom, the Moabites Chemosh and the Edomites Qaus (cf. Judg. 11.24; Deut. 32.8). The reduction of the pantheons undertaken in several cultures at the end of the second and the beginning of the first millennium severely limited the sociomorphic structure of the world of the gods known from Ugarit and thus the possibility of narrative myths.

Already more relevant is the question of what kind of chief deity (where there is one) a culture has, whether this is a storm god, as in individual Aramaean tribes, or a sun god, as in Egypt. At least from Deuteronomy 4 on, what is typical of the God of Israel is that more strongly than with any other ancient Near Eastern deities it is felt that none of these phenomena are adequate manifestations of him, probably because originally he was a storm god and god of war, but in Jerusalem took on features of a sun god. At the latest from the sixth century, more than with other deities of the ancient Near East he is imagined as being behind and above all phenomena (cf. Ezek. 1), though we should remember that even the sun god was never simply thought of as being identical with the sun. The sun was at best one of his forms. But Yahweh did not reveal himself to his worshippers in phenomena as his forms, but as his creatures.

Exegesis governed by dialectical theology thought it especially typical that Yahweh did not reveal himself in nature but in history. The question is whether there was already a notion comparable to our 'history' in the ancient Near East. It was a current notion accepted all over the Near East that deities were essentially involved in what on the surface were human actions, like wars. The reduction in the formation of myths mentioned above led here to a dangerous mythicizing of historial entities (Israel as people and land seen as Yahweh's consort, Israel's political opponents as powers of chaos).

What is typical of Yahweh and more original is the image of a god which came into being from aspects of a storm god and a sun god, a god who in his supremacy over the world is a militant champion of law and righteousness. This image of divine righteousness is matched, for example, in the royal psalms by that of the triumphant earthly ruler which is already presented in so impressive a way on Egyptian temple walls and Assyrian palace reliefs. But it is typical that this potent ancient Near Eastern complex of notions was combined in Israel with a political tradition in which power was not transferred to a kingship which had come down from heaven, but to a kingship which had come into being through treaties (II Sam. 5.3) and remained open to criticism (I Kings 12). This fundamental contestability of any human power which Yahweh legitimated (I Sam. 12; Deut. 17) and the eschatological proviso associated with it, which reserves for God alone any form of final rule, are contributions to the culture of humankind which have not been handed down to us in this form by any Near Eastern culture and which still have lost nothing of their topicality. Where Christian great powers succumbed to the delusion that their rule represented the kingdom of God, whether in Byzantium, among the Catholic kings and queens of Spain in the fifteenth and sixteenth centuries or in the Czarist Russia of the nineteenth century, Judaism was always exposed to particularly brutal persecutions. By its mere existence it gave the lie to the blasphemous illusion that the kingdom of God had been made present, and with blood and tears preserved the divinity of God and the freedom of human beings from any form of idolatry.

Translated by John Bowden

Note

The topics covered in this article are discussed at more length in my commentary on the Song of Songs (details in the notes on contributors below), and two articles which are in preparation: 'Sturmgott – Sonnengott – Einziger. Ein neuer Versuch die Enstehung des judäischen Monotheismus historisch zu verstehen', *Bibel und Kirche*, Stuttgart 49/2, 1994; 'Der zu hohe Preis der Identität oder von den schmerzlichen Beziehungen zwischen Christentum, Judentum und kanaanäischer Religion', in M. Dietrich and O. Loretz (eds.), *Ugarit – ein ostmediterranes Kulturzentrum im Alten Orient. Ergebnisse und Perspektiven der Forschung* (lectures given at the European Colloquium, 11–12 February 1993), Abhandlungen zur Literatur Alt-Syrien-Palästinas 7, Münster 1994.

Jews and Greeks: The Diaspora as an Experience of Cultural Diversification

Jacques van Ruiten

In 333 BCE Alexander the Great began his conquest of the East. After the centuries-long domination of the scene by Eastern empires like Assyria (900–612), Babylon (612–539) and Persia (539–333), now for the first time the whole of the East came under a Western sphere of influence. This resulted in a dissemination of Greek culture and brought with it great changes in politics, religion and culture for the people living there. The cultural and economic foundations of this Greek world civilization, which is called Hellenism, also continued, albeit with some changes, through the whole period of Roman domination.

One special feature of the Hellenistic period in the historical framework of the Jewish people is the existence of a widespread Jewish Diaspora. Although this Diaspora had already come into being earlier, particularly in the Babylonian period, in the course of the Hellenistic period it spread vigorously, and Jews became established in all the lands around the Mediterranean Sea. They were attracted by the great prosperous Hellenistic centres of population for economic and cultural reasons. The conquests of Palestine by the Ptolemies and the Seleucids had resulted in many of them being carried off as prisoners or slaves. Finally, internal Jewish social and political tensions led to the flight of many Jews to Egypt. Round the beginning of our era, more Jews were living abroad than in Palestine, and often in regions which were under Hellenistic influence.

Many Jews vigorously opposed the influence of Hellenism on their culture, as is most evident from the Maccabaean wars in the first half of the second century BCE. They tried to hold on to their own cultural and religious identity. But even Judaism succumbed to the influence of Hellenism, and this process took place not just in the Diaspora but also in

Palestine. Knowledge of the Greek language spread markedly among the Jews from the third century BCE on. Hellenistic forms of life (clothing, theatre-going and so on) were adopted, and Hellenistic forms of architecture came into their own. Knowledge of Greek literature, philosophy and religion also rapidly entered the Jewish sphere in Palestine and beyond.

In this article I shall concentrate on the question how Jewish literature in the early Hellenistic period reflects the cultural milieu in which it came into being. We shall first look at the Jewish writers who lived in Alexandria, paying attention above all to the historian Artapanus. Then we shall examine the situation in Palestine, where we shall be particularly occupied with the story of the treachery of the angels (I Enoch 6–11).

The Greek translation of the Torah

Alexandria above all exercised a great power of attraction on many Jews in the early Hellenistic period, not only because it was the greatest mercantile city but also because it was the centre of science and the arts. This city was the spiritual centre of the Hellenistic world. The very many Jews in this city who spoke Greek could not escape its influence. So they developed their own intellectual tradition, which was to last for centuries. By adopting Greek culture they tried to penetrate the privileged class of the Greeks and obtain equal status, while at the same time wanting to preserve their own Jewish identity.

The Greek translation of the Torah stood at the beginning of this tradition. The situation of Jews in Alexandria was such that already in the first half of the third century BCE many no longer knew Hebrew, so a need arose for a Greek translation of the Torah. The legend about the origin of this translation which has been preserved, for example, in the *Letter of Aristeas*, relates how seventy-two men, in silence and isolation, translated the Torah in seventy-two days. This translation has come to be known as the Septuagint (= Greek seventy) as a result. In the second and first century BCE the rest of the Hebrew Bible was then translated into Greek, part of it in Palestine.

The intention of the Septuagint is to render the Hebrew original as faithfully as possible. But at various places in this translation we come upon traces of Hellenistic thought-material. One could point to Genesis 1.2, where the Hebrew text reads 'the earth was desolate and empty'. The Septuagint translates here 'the earth was invisible and unordered'. This terminology is related to Greek philosophical ideas about the pre-existence of formless material, which has to be ordered by form, of the kind that we find in Plato (*Timaeus* 51a). In Exodus 3.14 God identifies himself to Moses as 'I am who I am'. This is rendered by the translators of the Septuagint 'I am the One who is.' The accord with Greek philosophy consists in the fact that the divine is seen as Being *par excellence*, in other words the unchangeable as contrasted to the material world of coming to be and passing away. The Greek translation of Proverbs 8.22–31, the well-known passage about God's Wisdom, deviates markedly from the Hebrew original. Thus wisdom was created as the beginning of God's work. To the degree that she is present at creation, she guarantees the harmony of perfection and beauty. This notion of wisdom shows various agreements with the idea of the 'world soul' in Plato and later in the Stoa.

Alexandrian Jewish literature

The influence of Greek culture on Alexandrian Judaism is expressed not only in the Greek translation of the Bible but also in the writings of Jewish authors. Most of this literature has been lost, but from the fragments which have been preserved we can see that Jews wrote in various Greek literary genres. Thus the Jewish historian Demetrius wrote a chronological work *On the Kings of the Jews*, in the style of Greek scientific chronography of the end of the third century BCE, the purpose of which was to demonstrate the very great antiquity of the national Jewish tradition. He was followed in the second century by historians like Artapanus and Cleodemus Malchus. Greek epic poetry was written by poets like Philo the Elder, who composed his work in hexameters; the Samaritan Theodotus; and the author of the third book of the Sibylline oracles, while the playwright Ezekiel the Tragedian was capable of writing his work in iambic trimeters. They sketch what is certainly an apologetic picture of Jewish history, but at the same time do not reject the use of examples from Greek mythology. We find the first philosophical literature in Aristobulus. He combines Greek philosophical systems, above all those of Pythagoras, Plato and some of the Stoics, with Jewish traditions, above all the wisdom traditions as we find them in the books of Proverbs, Ben Sirach and the Wisdom of Solomon. The climax of the Alexandrian Jewish tradition came with Philo of Alexandria (10 BCE – 40 CE). He saw himself as a Greek and a Jew at the same time. His synthesis between Greek philosophy, above all that of Plato, and the Jewish tradition, can be seen in his view of the logos as mediating between God and the world.

Artapanus

Here, by way of illustration, we shall investigate more closely one of these Jewish writers from Alexandria, the historian Artapanus, who lived in the second century BCE. Three fragments of his work have been preserved. These deal with the heroic acts of three forefathers of the Jewish people, namely Abraham, Joseph and Moses. The story that Artapanus sketches differs in various respects from the biblical text. Thus in the first fragment Abraham instructs the Egyptians in astrology, while in the second fragment Joseph voluntarily goes to Egypt and is immediately appointed governor there. There is no mention of any incident with Potiphar's wife and of his time in prison. Joseph is said to have been the first to have organized a just division of the land; and he is also said to have invented measures. The third fragment is extensive and is concerned with Moses. Great inventions are also attributed to him, like shipbuilding, machines for lifting heavy stones, the irrigation system, weapons and philosophy. In addition he divided the land into thirty-six districts and set over each district the deity whom it had to worship (cats, dogs, ibisis). These benefactions made Moses popular among the masses; the Egyptian priests showed him divine honours and he was called Hermes, i.e. Thoth, the Egyptian god of culture and science. According to Artapanus Moses (in Greek *Mooüsēs*) was called by the Greeks *Mooüsos*, the teacher of the mythical singer Orpheus. In Greek mythology the relationship between Orpheus and Musaeus is the other way round: Orpheus is the teacher of Musaeus. The reversal of the relationship by Artapanus contributes to the glorification of Moses. Moreover, in this way Moses is indirectly seen as the founder of Greek culture. According to tradition (Herodotus, Plato, Hecataeus), Orpheus is the one who brought culture and religion from Egypt to the Greeks.

Because Moses was so popular among the people, he incurred the hatred of Pharaoh, who sent him on a campaign against the Ethiopians. Here, however, Moses was unexpectedly successful. After that Moses killed a man who was sent to murder him and fled to Arabia. He later returned to Egypt to bring about the liberation of the Hebrews. Then he ended up in prison, but the doors opened of their own accord, after which Moses entered the palace. The king was disconcerted by this and thereupon asked Moses to tell him the name of his God. The rest of the story, finally, describes the plagues and the exodus through the Red Sea and remains quite close to the biblical text.

The reason why Artapanus' work diverges so markedly from the biblical story must be sought in the fact that like the other Hellenistic Jewish writers he was strongly influenced by the anti-Jewish historiography of Egyptian authors, of whom Manetho from the third century BCE is the best known. These practised the literary genre of 'rival' historiography. In this genre the superiority of one's own people and religion was emphasized. So it was that Manetho increased the glory of Egypt by belittling the Jews and telling negative stories about their origin. The early Jewish authors did not defend themselves directly, but tried to defeat their opponents with their own weapons namely by making use of the same literary genre of rival historiography, with the aim of emphasizing the superiority of Moses, and thus of the Jewish people and their religion. These inventions, which were of great cultural importance in the Hellenistic period and were attributed to legendary heroes, are now attributed to the Jewish forefathers Abraham, Joseph and above all Moses. In this way they in fact became Jewish inventions. Moreover many cultures, including Greek culture, were made dependent on Moses. Various themes in Artapanus's work (for example the initiation of animal worship and Moses' Ethiopian campaign) run parallel to themes from the work of Manetho and seem intended as implicit refutations of it.

There are further Hellenistic motifs in the work of Artapanus which also appear in connection with the Dionysus and which could indicate that Artapanus was writing against the cult of Dionysus in Alexandria, in which Jews, too, were forced to take part (cf. III Macc. 2.29–31). Here I would refer simply to the motif of the prison door opening by itself. The god Dionysus is also freed in this way. This motif of the miraculous freeing of the hero recurs many times in ancient literature and has also found its way into the New Testament (cf. Acts 5.17–25; 12.6–17), but it does not occur elsewhere in Jewish literature.

It has been pointed out that Artapanus, like other early Jewish Hellenistic historians, pays no attention to the Torah as a law book. For early Hellenistic Judaism Moses is the wise man, the inventor and the great leader, but not the lawgiver. This could mean that part of early Hellenistic Judaism thought of its identity not in terms of the law, like later rabbinic Judaism, but in stories about its forefathers in which they proved to be superior to the Greek and Egyptian heroes. That in this defence of ancestral traditions writers sometimes went against these traditions, as in the description of Abraham as the inventor of astrology and of Moses as the founder of Egyptian animal worship, and moreover made use of Hellenistic traditions, is characteristic of the new cultural sitution in which Judaism moved.

Palestine

In the post-exilic period Palestinian Judaism produced a rich and many-sided literature. This reflects the many-sidedness of Judaism in the early Hellenistic period. Here we must realize that virtually none of the literature of the pro-Hellenistic minority of Palestine has survived the course of events associated with the Maccabean revolt. To what degree Hellenistic influence has determined the composition and redaction of the Old Testament writings is disputed, but it certainly cannot be excluded in the late wisdom literature, like Proverbs 1–9. The apocryphal and pseudepigraphical literature often makes use of literary forms which also occur in the Greek language sphere, like historiography (e.g. I Maccabees, Jubilees, the Genesis Apocryphon), letters (e.g. the Letter of Jeremiah and the Apocalypse of Baruch) and romanticized narratives (e.g. Tobit and Judith), but the agreements with literary forms from their own Jewish tradition are so great that it is difficult to speak of a demonstrable Hellenistic influence.

That does not detract from the fact that in Palestine, too, early in the Hellenistic period, in reflection on their own Jewish tradition, authors at the same time made use of elements from Hellenistic traditions. Early witnesses to this are Pseudo-Eupolemus, an anonymous Samaritan historian, and Eupolemus, the member of a leading priestly family and a supporter of the Maccabaean policy. Both wrote in Greek in the first half of the second century BCE, and both show various agreements with Artapanus, who was discussed earlier. They are very free over the biblical texts, which they adapt at will in an attempt to make the biblical tradition correspond with non-Jewish historiography. To this end they refer back to Greek writers, who were evidently being read in Palestine. In an attempt to strengthen their own self-awareness, important cultural inventions are attributed to their own forefathers. Enoch was the inventor of astrology, in which Abraham then instructed the other peoples. Moses is the inventor of writing, as a result of which the Torah became the oldest of all books. Here finally the whole of Hellenism could be made dependent on Moses.

The treachery of the angels (I Enoch 6–11)

It is striking that Hellenistic influence can also be demonstrated in literature which came into being in the circle of Hasidim (the 'pious'), who were strictly opposed to Hellenism. One example of this is the story of the treachery of the angels in I Enoch 6–11, which probably comes from the first half of the second century BCE. The story is on the one hand rooted in biblical tradition, but on the other makes use of mythological material from the Hellenistic world to direct it against the Hellenistic overlords.

Central to the story of I Enoch 6–11 is the lament over a world which is full of injustice and corruption. This evil is attributed to the treachery of the angels. They are responsible for the violence of the giants, whom they aroused by doing violence to the daughters of men; for the fabrication of weapons of war, for unchastity; and for the spread of secret divine knowledge like magic and soothsaying among the human race. The rebellious angels finally suffered divine judgment.

The story of I Enoch 6–11 comprises the oldest and at the same time the most thorough reworking of Gen. 6.1–4 in the post-biblical literature. Thus Genesis 6.1–2 is taken over completely: 'In those days, when the children of man had multiplied, it happened that there were born unto them handsome and beautiful daughters. And the angels, the children of heaven, saw them and desired them; and they said to one another, "Come, let us choose wives for ourselves from among the daughters of men and beget us children"' (I Enoch 6.1–2). The text of Gen. 6.4 is also recognizable with a few changes: 'And they took wives unto themselves, and everyone (respectively) chose one woman for himself, and they began to go unto them . . . And the women became pregnant and gave birth to great giants . . . ' (I Enoch 7.1–2). The author of I Enoch does not include a number of phrases from Gen. 6.4 ('and also afterward', 'of old', 'men of renown'), and he identifies the 'men of renown' with the 'giants'. The way in which he takes over large parts of Gen. 6.1–4 almost literally gives the impression that he has taken over an old Jewish tradition and is developing it further.

However, careful study of the text shows that the small changes that the author makes in his rendering of Gen. 6.4 have important consequences. Thus the identification of 'men of renown' with 'giants' reverses the intention of the Genesis story. Genesis 6.4 describes how from a voluntary union of the gods with human women men of renown (who are seen in a positive light) emerge to fight with the giants, who were already on earth. By contrast, in I Enoch it is said that no men of renown emerged from these unions, which are now seen negatively, but 'giants'. The giants are negative figures who are present only to the detriment of human beings and even destroy them.

Strikingly enough, the anti-Hellenistic author of I Enoch 6–11 combines the 'transformed' text of Gen. 6.1–4 with a Hellenistic tradition which reports the betrayal of heavenly secrets to human beings. This tradition is known as the Prometheus saga, fragments of which have been preserved in the works of the Greek authors Hesiod and Aeschylus.

Prometheus is wise and intelligent and uses his wisdom to help human beings. However, by doing this he rebels against Zeus, for which he is punished. Moreover his beneficence to humankind ultimately proves to be the fundamental source of evil in the world. According to the story all human skills come from Prometheus. Its best-known feature is that Prometheus steals fire and gives this to human beings, but he also instructs them in woodworking, housebuilding, the rising of stars and their positions, numbers and letters, the taming of animals, medicines and the interpretation of dreams and the flight of birds. As punishment for his rebellion against Zeus Prometheus is sent into the wilderness, where he is chained hand and foot. When he continues his accusations against the supreme god, Zeus makes the rock open and Prometheus is swallowed up until a later time, when he will be subjected to a horrifying torture.

The author of I Enoch 6–11 does not take over the story of the Prometheus saga literally. But his text shows so many points of sometimes unique correspondence with this saga that dependence on it must be thought to be very probable. As in the Prometheus saga, in I Enoch 6–11 a heavenly being (Azael) rebels against God by teaching and revealing certain things to human beings. The focusing of these revealed things on the mining and working of metals intensifies the parallelism with Prometheus's theft of fire, because fire is essential for working metals. For this rebellious act, like Prometheus, he is bound hand and foot and cast into the wilderness. Like the Prometheus saga, I Enoch reports that the earth opens and swallows up the main figure until a later time, when punishment will be inflicted.

In I Enoch the instruction in metalworking ends up with the manufacture of jewels, which make women seductive. Then the women seduce the angel Shemyaz and his helpers. This is the beginning of all evil. In the Prometheus saga, after Prometheus has instructed human beings, Zeus sends an attractive and seductive woman (Pandora), who is bedecked with gold and ornaments, bearing a box full of gifts and evils. When she opens this, the evils fly out over humankind.

Scholars have pointed out a hidden allusion in I Enoch to one of the works of Hesiod, his *Works and Days*. The Prometheus myth has been preserved in this work. In I Enoch 12.2 Enoch says: 'And his works were with the watchers/ and with the holy ones were his days.' The pairing of works and days is strange in synonymous parallelism, and does not occur elsewhere in the Bible or related literature. In connection with the title of Hesiod's work it could indicate a direct dependence of I Enoch on this work.

I could go on to point out other Greek myths which are reflected in the

story of I Enoch 6–11. However, this reference to the Prometheus myth
has shown that already in an early phase of the history of Hellenism there
was a thorough knowledge of Greek mythology, even in Palestine. Thus
even traditional Jewish literature already reflects at an early period the
Hellenistic milieu in which it came into being.

Conclusion

The central question posed by this article was how Jewish literature from
the early Hellenistic period reflects the cultural milieu in which it came
into being. I have demonstrated that Judaism in this period was many-
sided. There were divergent trends, each of which reacted in its own way
to the new social and cultural reality. They extended from an eager
embrace of Hellenistic culture to total opposition to it. The literary
evidence from this period proves on the one hand to be powerfully
opposed to the influence of Hellenism on Jewish culture (for example the
author of I Enoch 6–11) and at the same time to be deeply influenced by
it. On the other hand, the evidence shows that even those who were
positive towards the new culture wanted to maintain their Jewish identity
and that in their own way they remained faithful to the Jewish tradition. I
pointed out in my discussion of the historiographer Artapanus that
holding on to one's own tradition sometimes means going against this
same tradition in a creative way. So different forms of new Jewish
identity came into being in this period. Finally, we can see that the
Jewish biblical tradition was evidently strong enough in the early Hellenistic period to cope with the new cultural situation. At the same time it
shows an openness which made it possible for new and sometimes strong
influences from outside to renew it without really threatening the ongoing
existence of Judaism.

Translated by John Bowden

Select Bibliography

R. Bartelmus, *Heroentum in Israel und seiner Umwelt*, Abhandlungen zur
Theologie des Alten und Neuen Testaments 65, Zurich 1979.
J. H. Charlesworth, *The Old Testament Pseudepigrapha* II, New York and
London 1985.
Compendia Rerum Iudaicarum ad Novum Testamentum, Assen 1974ff. (a multi-
volume series).
M. Hengel, *Judaism and Hellenism*, London and Philadelphia 1974.

P. W. van der Horst, *Ancient Jewish Epitaphs. An Introductory Survey of a Millennium of Jewish Funerary Epigraphy (300 BCE to 700 CE)*, Contributions to Biblical Exegesis and Theology 2, Kampen 1991.

—, *Studies over het jodendom in de oudheid*, Kampen 1992.

E. Schürer, *The History of the Jewish People in the Age of Jesus Christ (175 BC–AD 135). A New English Version Revised and Edited by Geza Vermes and Fergus Millar*, I–III, Edinburgh 1973–1987.

S. Talmon (ed.), *Jewish Civilization in the Hellenistic-Roman Period*, Journal for the Study of the Pseudepigrapha, Supplement Series 10, Sheffield 1991.

G. Veltri, *Eine Tora für den König Talmai*, Texte und Studien zum Antiken Judentum 41, Tübingen 1994.

N. Walter, *Artapanos*, Jüdische Schriften aus hellenistisch-römischer Zeit I/2, Gütersloh 1976.

'Telling in Their Own Tongues': Old and Modern Bible Translations as Expressions of Ethnic Cultural Identity

Willard G. Oxtoby

Three things, say many anthropologists, distinguish human beings from other creatures: tool-making, abstract language and religion. Tool-making has now become a differentiating feature among cultures, bringing some parts of the world into a high-tech society, the envy of the remainder. And part of the reason human culture is so rich and diverse is that both languages and religions are also differentiated, existing in great variety.

While the diversity of languages constitutes a great cultural treasure, it also serves as an obstacle to the primary function of language, which is communication. Language is an inextricable combination of content with form, and the forms are necessarily specific to particular languages. Therein lie some of the challenges and problems relating to translation.

Is the translator (Latin *traductor*) a traitor (*traditor*)? There are philosophers who assert that accurate translation from one language into another is impossible. And many students of literature and of vocal music are aware of texts that lose their depth or their beauty in translation. But in a linguistically diverse world we have no alternative to the enterprise of translation and must use it, with all its limitations.

This does not mean that all religions eagerly make use of translation. On the whole, religious traditions tend to be conservative in their worship and in their scriptures. Some flourished in a self-contained area among a specific population. Tribal and ancient national religions might privilege that population, or a hereditary priestly élite within it. Such traditions experienced little need for translation. They could even make their linguistic homogeneity a cornerstone of faith. In such traditions, the ancient language of the prayers, often also recorded in classic texts, is 'frozen' as the language of ritual and of authority. The idea of Shinto using any language other than Japanese is hard to grasp. Brahmin priests intone the Hindu rituals in Sanskrit, always a formal more than a vernacular language. Orthodox Jews maintain their liturgy in Hebrew, Zoroastrians in the ancient Iranian language of the Avesta, and so on.

Hence we may fail to recognize what a relatively new departure it was for a religion to employ translation to the extent that Christianity, with universal aspirations, did from its inception two thousand years ago. In this article we explore some of the experiences and some of the implications of the translation process, dwelling especially on the Bible and its translations. And we shall do so within a comparative perspective that does not ignore the experiences of the other great religions of the world.

1. Translation within biblical times

Linguistic diversity is one of the problems of human existence which the Bible mentions in its narratives of origins. Just as toil and drudgery are among the consequences of Adam and Eve's hubris in Eden, so the confusion of tongues is presented as a punishment for building an ambitious ziggurat in Babylon, referred to by tradition as the Tower of Babel.

As the eleventh chapter of Genesis tells the story, God is alarmed that the people engaged in this building project plan for its top to reach the heavens. He observes that this ambition is only the beginning of what humans will try to do, nothing being impossible for them. So not only does God confuse their language to abort the project, but he scatters them across the face of the earth. Babel (in Hebrew the name of Babylon but also associated with *balal*, 'to confuse') has come primarily to signify linguistic chaos, but the story also explicitly associates the event with geographical dispersal.

But linguistic diversity as a problem operated on a much more intimate scale during the early stages of Israel's tribal and national existence. In the period of the conquest and settlement of Canaan, the principal linguistic diversity that the Israelites encountered was at the level of dialect difference, not language difference. Neighbouring populations spoke on the whole in ways which while noticeably different, were still mutually intelligible, as for instance Australian English and American English are today. On dialect as a test of identity, Judges 12 recounts how the men of

Gilead under Jephthah's leadership detected Ephraimite infiltrators crossing the river Jordan by asking them to pronounce the word for a running stream, *shibboleth*. If someone said *sibboleth*, his dialect exposed him as a fugitive from Ephraim, and the text reports that 42,000 Ephraimites were slain.

We are now in a position to reconsider the Tower of Babel story. In my view, the historical situation that it illustrates is not the age of primaeval ancestors or of Israelite national origins but a much later period: the time of the Babylonian Exile after the collapse of the Judean kingdom in the sixth century BCE. At that point, the Babylonians deported the leadership element of the conquered Judeans to Mesopotamia, a distance of 800 km (500 miles). In that setting, removed from their homeland, the Hebrews truly did encounter a confusion of tongues. To them the Babylonian speech was much less intelligible than the dialects of neighbouring tribes in the Levant, even if Aramaic had made some headway as a trade language both in Palestine and in Babylonia. Moreover, the biblical account of the Tower of Babel includes the scattering of populations as part of God's punishment. So in the time of the Babylonian exile, this narrative served to account for the social and linguistic disruption experienced in long-range deportation. Presumably it also took note of dilapidated ziggurats on the Babylonian scene, some already two thousand years old.

Life in the Diaspora (dispersal), away from the Promised Land, has been a feature of Jewish experience ever since the Babylonian exile. Fifty years after the exile began, the conquest of Babylon by the Persian king, Cyrus, permitted the return of the surviving exiles and their descendants, but not all went back. Some who had been taken to Babylon or had fled elsewhere remained abroad, absorbing the diverse languages of their new homes. And while Hebrew remained the language of Jewish liturgy and scripture, it ceased to be the vernacular even in Palestine, where Aramaic replaced it.

The Jews who settled in Egypt, particularly in Alexandria from the fourth century BCE onwards, adopted Greek styles of architecture and dress and Greek names. Most lost the ability to read Hebrew. Hence, early in the third century BCE, a Greek translation of the Hebrew scriptures was made. It is known as the Septuagint, from the Latin word for 'seventy'. The circumstances of its production are reported in a legend in the *Letter of Aristeas*. According to the legend, seventy scholars sat down to the task of translating the Hebrew Bible into Greek and independently produced for King Ptolemy II Philadelphos seventy identical drafts.

Far from raising a suspicion of plagiarism, total agreement of the seventy efforts was hailed as a miracle, a sign of divine guidance. And since the Almighty had guided the hand of the translators, surely the translations were as authoritative as the Hebrew original. Judaism coped with language change and linguistic diversity by endorsing both the activity and the product of translation. Jews who spoke Greek used the Septuagint (and Jews who spoke Aramaic the Targums, a name meaning 'translations' in Aramaic) in study for access to the content of the tradition rather than using Hebrew for memorization of its form.

But translation brought the Bible into a whole new set of cultural expectations. Instead of reading it as the charter document of the Hebrew covenant community, Jews in Alexandria treated their Greek Bible more as an object of literary reflection. In Greek, the three divisions of Hebrew scripture, namely, Law, Prophets and Writings, were reshuffled into four: Law, history, poetry and prophecy. Essentially, the historical and poetical books that appeared in the Prophets and the Writings were sorted into new genre categories. It is thus that the books of Kings, which in Hebrew had been in the prophetic collection, and the priestly re-writing of them, Chronicles, from the Writings, came to be placed side by side, with their discrepancies the more evident through their juxtaposition.

In rendering the Hebrew text, the Septuagint translators had one foot in the graphic and physical style of the Hebrew and their other foot in the philosophical concerns of Greek culture. The Old Testament speaks of God in very human imagery, with hands, face, and so on. To some extent the Septuagint appears uncomfortable with this, and chooses more abstract language, resisting anthropomorphisms. I regard this as a philosophical preference of the translators, not a structural limitation of the capacity of either language to express thought.

When we move from language structure to the semantic range of individual vocabulary items, however, we find ample evidence of shifts in meaning when Hebrew is translated into Greek. This is because the specificity or ambiguity of a term in one language may not match the sense of the available translation term in the other. The Immanuel prophecy in Isaiah 7 is an excellent case in point. The Hebrew of Isaiah 7.14 sees a young woman as conceiving and bearing a son, whose name means 'God is with us'. As is well known, the Hebrew word means 'young woman', and a different Hebrew word is commonly used for 'virgin'. But in the Greek, the term chosen is ambiguous and permits the meaning 'virgin', opening up the possibility for Matthew to interpret Mary's virginity as a fulfilment of Isaiah 7.14.

There are many other instances within the Bible where the New

Testament quotes the Old Testament and does so in translation. Hebraic
and Hellenic outlooks on the structure of human personality are in contrast
when Jesus cites the central affirmation of Jewish faith, the *Shema* of
Deuteronomy 6. Asked which is the greatest commandment, he responds
with this affirmation, which declares that the Lord is one and commands
the love of God with all of one's being. In the Hebrew, that is expressed as
leb (heart or mind), *nephesh* (self or soul), and *me'od* (strength or might).
While Matthew, the Gospel writer who most frequently quotes the Old
Testament, uses three terms to cite the passage in Deuteronomy, Mark
12.30 and Luke 10,27 both specify four: heart, soul, mind and strength. In
Hebrew, one 'thinks' in one's 'heart'. But mind and heart are clearly more
distinguishable in Hellenic psychology, where one becomes intellect and
the other emotion.

2. Translation and the expansion of Christianity

I have mentioned the Jewish legendary account that takes the resemblance
among seventy Septuagint translations to be providential rather than mere
coincidence. But validating translation by miracle was not something
unique to Judaism. For the Christians, a comparable validation was the
Pentecost experience of the apostolic church. Fifty days after the first
Easter, as Luke tells the story in the second chapter of Acts, the circle of
Jesus' followers experience the gift of the Holy Spirit as tongues of fire that
enable them to preach the gospel in diverse languages. Unlike the tongue-
speaking that goes on in charismatic Christianity today, the charisma of
Pentecost was intelligible speech. The Pentecost account, which validated
translation for the church's mission, represents a spiritual gift of communication, not of performance.

From the earliest times, Christianity employed translation to spread its
message. The earliest Christians were Jews whose scriptural and liturgical
language was Hebrew, the former language of the small tribal kingdoms.
But ever since the Babylonian exile six centuries earlier, as we have seen,
Aramaic, widely used in trade from Egypt all the way to Persia, had been
the day-to-day language of Jews in Palestine. Then Greek became the
language of trade and of learning around the eastern Mediterranean, and
now Latin was the language of the new Roman rulers of the area.
Missionary activity by Christians would thus require a minimum of three
languages: Aramaic (which with Christian vocabulary became Syriac),
Greek and Latin. These would by no means be the only Christian
languages, but identities forged on the basis of these three came to
represent the three principal divisions of the first millennium of Christian-

ity: the oriental churches of Persia and Central Asia such as the Nestorians, with Syriac as their scriptural and liturgical language; the Byzantine church with Greek; and the Roman Catholic church with Latin.

Within the boundaries of the Roman empire, Christians used Greek and Latin. These two languages were already well established, with a high culture and a well-developed literary and rhetorical tradition. If anything, the New Testament was popular writing in comparison with the established classics, being in *koine* (common) Greek, and scholars of classical studies since the Renaissance have often spurned it as Greek literature.

The Bible in Latin came to have a more fortunate status as literature, thanks to the efforts of the fourth-century Jerome. With Christianity newly established as the imperial religion, the intellectual resources of Roman culture were being enlisted in the service of the faith. Like his contemporary Augustine, Jerome had an education in classical rhetoric. So Jerome's Latin translation of the Bible, while called the Vulgate because it was in the language of the common people, was a product of some literary skill. It stood as the standard Latin version as long as Latin remained the language of learning throughout Western Europe.

In Europe beyond the frontiers of the Roman empire, the languages of the Goths and others lacked any substantial written literature. The Christians were – to use a Muslim term – 'people of the book', which meant that the spread of Christianity in northern and eastern Europe brought the spread of writing and of literary study. In pagan northern and eastern Europe, the advent of Christian liturgy and scriptures often constituted the first taste of literacy. Along with the technique of writing, the Christian contribution has offered models for literary style and a fund of cultural ideas and ideals. The Bible was translated into the language of the Goths in the fourth century by Ulfilas, a man of Gothic parentage who lived in Constantinople and then returned to preach Christianity among his people. In the mid-ninth century, two brothers, Cyril and Methodius, took Byzantine Christianity to Moravia, the region of the Czech republic today, where Cyril devised an alphabet (termed Cyrillic after him) in which to write the Slavonic language, based on the forms of letters in Greek.

Language was particularly important in the Byzantine missionary efforts among the Slavic peoples. Though the Byzantines used Greek within their empire, they used local vernaculars in their missionary activity beyond the imperial frontier. This encouraged the development of independent local churches with a strong sense of national identity based on language. The Cyrillic alphabet, with liturgy and scripture in Slavic languages, became the norm for Byzantine converts among the Slavs, to this day mainly Orthodox, such as Bulgarian, Serbian, Ukrainian and Russian. Romania, originally colonized by Rome as the province of Dacia, was Christian from the fourth century and uses a Latin alphabet, but its church later came into the Eastern Orthodox orbit during Bulgarian rule.

Meanwhile, Roman Catholic missionaries reached other Slavic peoples, maintaining a Latin liturgy and a Bible in Latin in keeping with more centralized church control and spreading the Latin alphabet. Thus Latin characters are used to write languages of the dominantly Catholic Slavic peoples, such as the Croats, Slovenes, Czechs, Slovaks, Poles, Lithuanians and Latvians. The Hungarians, also mainly Catholic, use the Latin alphabet too, but for a language that is not of the Slavic group.

Rome's efforts to recruit the allegiance of Christians in the Eastern Orthodox world subsequently produced the bodies known as Uniate churches. The name, first used by those who disapproved of the connection, derives from the Union of Brest-Litovsk, east of Warsaw, in 1595, when the Ruthenian church of the Ukraine affiliated with Rome. Other unions with churches of the Byzantine rite included Hungarians in 1595, Yugoslavs in 1611, Romanians in 1701, Melkites in the Levant in 1724, and Bulgars and Greeks in 1860. Compromise with Eastern usage was the order of the day as Rome sought satellites in the Eastern Christian world. Besides retaining married clergy, the Uniate churches enjoyed the concession to use their national languages that Eastern Orthodoxy had brought.

But language and nationality as markers of identity bring costs as well as benefits. Participation of Eastern European Christians in religious services during the Communist era after the mid-twentieth century was one way by which sentiment against Soviet domination could be expressed. But when the Communist order collapsed in 1989, linguistic and ethnic identities became a major bone of contention, plunging formerly secular Yugoslavia into ethnic strife among Catholic Croats, Orthodox Serbs and Muslim Bosnians.

Ironically, Latin Christianity came to resist translation of scripture and liturgy in the mediaeval and early modern world. This was in part because Catholic missionaries encountered populations without substantial indigenous literatures, particularly in the sixteenth-century spread of Christianity in the Western hemisphere. In India and East Asia, however, Catholic missionaries encountered high cultures with sophisticated philosophies. When the Jesuits reached China near the end of the sixteenth century, there began a fascinating episode in which serious principles of religious understanding were at stake.

Essentially the Jesuits in China sought to base their appeal to the literate class upon the correspondences between their Christian message and the rich resources of Chinese intellectual and religious culture. Theirs was an enterprise of active cultural exchange, in which Chinese philosophical and religious texts were translated into Latin and other European languages, while translations into Chinese were done both for European mathematical and astronomical texts and for the Bible. However, the Jesuits were being challenged by rival Franciscans and Dominicans, whose mediaeval experience in Europe and recent experience in places like the Philippines had conditioned a harsh response towards anything that smacked of paganism. There were political reasons for complaint about the Jesuits to Rome, but there were also theological and intellectual issues at stake.

Central to our topic was the so-called 'terms controversy'. Should Chinese terms, such as *T'ien* (heaven) or *Shang-ti* (the Lord above), be used as equivalents for the Christian God? The implied choice was between equation and differentiation. Equating content, one can do as the Greeks and Romans happily did when they took Zeus to be the same deity as Jupiter and, for that matter, as Baal. The classical Hebraic alternative was to assert the absolute incompatibility of Yahweh with Baal or any other rival, but that meant that to say 'God' in Chinese would be to use a proper name rather than a translatable term.

Some, who feared assimilation, insisted on coining a new term rather than associating God with an extant Chinese one. They proposed *T'ien-chu* (Lord of heaven), but to the strictest Christians even this seemed too tied to Chinese thought. In a dialectical opposition to everything with Chinese content, the right-wing Christians brought into Chinese the Latin term for God, as a proper name in Chinese: *Deusu*. This is what the missionaries had called God in Japan, only to discover later that the sound in Japanese meant 'big lie' (*dai-usu*).

Martin Luther launched the Protestant Reformation in 1517 with a challenge to ecclesiastical authority on a number of issues relating to sin and redemption, using scripture and the inner guidance of the Holy Spirit as a fulcrum of authority for leverage against the institutional tradition, the *magisterium*, of the church. Luther's translation of the Bible into a direct, lively German was immensely influential.

Luther was by no means the first to seek to translate the Bible into late mediaeval Europe's emerging vernaculars. In twelfth-century Lyons, Pierre Valdès (Peter Waldo) and his followers translated Scripture into French. In fourteenth-century England John Wyclif sought to replace the Latin of the Bible and the liturgy with English, and among the Czechs John Hus proposed comparable moves for his language. But in the form it took, the Protestant Reformation could not have happened much earlier than it actually did. That is because the technology of printing from movable type was introduced in Europe only in 1456, when a Latin Bible came from Johann Gutenberg's press in Strasbourg. Following Gutenberg's achievement, printing was available to disseminate Luther's challenges – and his translations – more widely and more popularly than would have previously been envisioned.

The most recent major phase of Christian translation of scripture was associated with Protestant missions and began in the middle of the nineteenth century. By the mid-twentieth, the Bible had been translated into a thousand languages and dialects, principally of tribal populations in the lands colonized by Europeans. It is no wonder that in the mid-twentieth century the emerging discipline of linguistics gained much of its impetus from the field experience of missionaries among aboriginal peoples, for the missionaries were doing pioneer work in describing the phonetics, grammar and lexicon of languages previously unrecorded. Often the languages were oral only, so that the translator would have to adapt the Latin alphabet or devise another. Missionaries needed ingenuity to find cultural equivalents. For example, a felicitious translation of 'prophet' into the language of the Gbeapo people of Liberia turned out to be 'God's town crier'.

3. Scripture and translation among the world's religions

While spoken language is constantly in a process of change, scriptural and liturgical texts tend to freeze or anchor the usage of the moment when they were fixed in writing. The way in which the 1611 King James translation of the Bible served as a model for literature well into the nineteenth century is familiar to English speakers. By then, it had grown archaic, but Protestants clung to it passionately. The now archaic usage itself became a dialect reserved for religious contexts. Spoken English had substituted 'you' for 'thou' by the nineteenth century, but Protestant clergy throughout the English-speaking world continued to pray extemporaneously in King James English: 'wouldst Thou, O Lord . . . ' We know that such traditionalism would have dismayed the translators who produced the King James in the first place in 1611, because in their preface they give as a justification for their own project the argument that time does not stand still and the work of the past must be updated:

Blessed be they, and most honoured be their name, that break the ice, and give onset upon that which helpeth forward to the saving of souls . . . yet for all that, as nothing is begun and perfected at the same time, . . . we building upon their foundation that went before us, and being holpen by their labours, do endeavour to make that better which they left so good.

Religious tradition preserves not only the form of language but the form of books. The codex or bound volume, which replaced the scroll in Roman times, represented a distinct technological advance: one could quickly 'fast-forward' to any point on a much later page in a long text. Mediaeval Jewish manuscripts, including commentaries on the Bible and Talmud, were in codex form. But, while one might study a copy of the Pentateuch in bound form (called a *chumash*, from the Hebrew for 'five'), tradition to this day has maintained in scroll form the copies of the Torah kept in the synagogue and read during worship.

An important example of the stabilizing role of scripture in religious traditions is the role of the Qur'an in Islam. As the first book historically to be circulated in the Arabic of seventh-century western Arabia, it served as a literary and stylistic model in all the lands of the Arab Muslim conquest, where Arabic became the new vernacular. Its influence as a literary model is parallel to but even greater than Luther's translation of the Bible in German or Dante's *Divina Commedia* in Italian. The Qur'an actually has had a cementing influence on the Arabic language down to the present century. Even after fourteen centuries, a standard Arabic closer to the Qur'an than to daily speech unites the Arabic-speaking world by providing a common denominator of formal language, used for speeches and for all writing.

The Qur'an, which as a book includes the recitations made by Muhammad on different occasions, includes the divine declaration, 'Indeed We [i.e., God] have revealed it, a recitation in Arabic.' Islamic theology developed its understanding of the Qur'an as God's word by reasoning that it must be eternal, manifested in human experience at the time of its recitation by Muhammad. In this sense the notion of the Qur'an as revelation parallels the notion of Jesus as Logos or manifestation of eternal divine Word in John's Gospel. But if the Qur'an is eternal, then, according to Islamic theology, it must be in Arabic, and as such therefore untranslatable. Muslims understand a translation of the Qur'an to be no longer the Qur'an itself but an interpretation of it.

Besides Christianity and Islam, the other – and the oldest – of the world's three great missionary religions was Buddhism. It, too, experienced moments in which it resisted translation, and other moments, ultimately more numerous and influential, when it engaged in translation.

For about its first three centuries, Buddhism existed almost exclusively in an Indian milieu, with Sanskrit as the standard ritual and literary language of the Hindus. But the Buddhists wrote many of their texts in Pali, a kindred language closer to the speech of the people, functioning in relation to Sanskrit more or less as Italian did in relation to Latin, or the *koine* Greek of the New Testament in relation to classical Greek.

The conversion of the Indian king Ashoka to Buddhism in the third century BC had an effect comparable to Constantine's conversion to Christianity. Now Buddhism was an 'establishment' religion, and Ashoka took steps to spread it. Missionaries were sent to Sri Lanka and South-east Asia, lands which have remained Buddhist to this day, even though Buddhism died out in its Indian homeland. These missionary territories were largely without literatures, so that the texts in Pali remained established widely across the Theravada (southern) Buddhist world. With a largely monastic emphasis, Theravada could for some time maintain the use of Pali by religious specialists where Sinhalese, Thai, and other languages were the vernaculars. There is a resemblance to the role of Latin in the European Middle Ages.

Not too many centuries after Ashoka, another form of Buddhism, the teaching termed Mahayana, made its way from north-western India to Central Asia and thence to China. Even in Central Asia, Mahayana Buddhists translated their texts into local languages such as Sogdian, an Iranian language. Partly perhaps because Mahayana was a more populist or lay-oriented form of teaching than the Buddhism that earlier spread to the south and south-east, translation was the norm in this north-western and north-eastern phase of Buddhist expansion. The Chinese Buddhist canon was eventually a collection far longer than the Qur'an or the Bible. Far more extensive even than the Talmud, it was a library on the scale of the entire corpus of the Greek and Latin church fathers. In the sheer magnitude of the enterprise, given the number of texts and the conceptual differences between Indian and Chinese culture, the translation of Buddhism from Indian languages into Chinese is probably the most impressive single translation activity in the history of religions.

Like the form of the book in Western religions discussed above, we find a conservatism of form applying in the case of Buddhist scriptures as well. In ancient India, manuscripts were inscribed horizontally on long strips of palm leaf. A long text would be on many such leaves, pierced and bundled together with string. Such bundles were evidently stored in baskets, as the three parts of the Buddhist canon are termed the 'three baskets' (Tripitaka). But palm leaves were not an available commodity in the high country of Tibet. When Buddhism was carried there and the scriptures translated into Tibetan, the texts were engraved, page by page, on wooden blocks and copies printed on paper. The shape and layout of the pages remained horizontal, replicating the palm-leaf manuscript form of India. Printed copies of the Tibetan canon are still made in this form, even if other books now printed in Tibetan resemble European books in layout.

In both mediaeval Asia and Renaissance Europe the manuscript book gave way to the printed book. Printing facilitated access to scripture, making it a visual experience for many people instead of only an auditory one. In our times, the printed book is under threat from electronic communications technology. Christian reflection on the role of language and communication today may see a new confusion of tongues, a new Babel. But the opportunities for communication may also signal a new Pentecost, if we recognize that each age must reappropriate scripture afresh, translating it into contemporary vocabulary. In the Second Vatican Council, after which this journal was named, that was part of the meaning of *aggiornamento*.

'Neither Jew nor Greek': The Challenge of Building One Multicultural Religious Community

John K. Riches

What impelled early Christians to embark on the long and perilous task of trying to forge into a unified community people of different religious, ethnic and social background, not to mention people of different gender? What theological beliefs led them to undertake such a task? What strategies did they develop as they embarked on it? And a further question: to what extent in all this was Christianity drawing on cultural forces which were latent in its socio-cultural environment? To what extent was it bringing to the world of the first century new insights and strategies which would further such a task?

Such questions are not new. They were first raised pertinently and with astonishing vigour by the German Hegelian scholar Ferdinand Christian Baur, whose *Church History of the First Three Centuries*[1] appeared in 1853. It was the first of the modern historical presentations of the origins of Christianity, a work of surprising roundedness and authority which dominated New Testament studies for the rest of the century. Baur's fundamental claim was that Christianity represented a major advance in the developing consciousness of the world. As Rome developed its political and military control over the world, so 'the barriers raised by national sentiment had been broken down'. The time for the coming to birth of a more universal form of religion had arrived. 'The universalism of Christianity is essentially nothing but that universal form of consciousness at which the development of mankind had arrived at the time when Christianity arrived' (5). Christianity, however, does not spring fully grown from Judaism. There is a gradual process of transition from Jesus through Paul to the emergence of the early Catholic church. In Jesus there was on the one side the moral universal, the unconfined humanity, the divine exaltation which gave his person its absolute significance. On the other side 'there was the cramping and narrowing influence of the Jewish national Messianic idea' (49). Among Jesus' first followers after his death, too, there was tension between preoccupation with particular regulations and practices on the one hand and the universal spirit of the gospel on the other. Thus the conflict between Paul and Peter at Antioch, which is described in Gal. 2, represents a dialectic between two forces in Christianity: Paul's law-free gospel and Petrine Christianity with its observance of the Law. Out of the two comes a synthesis, early Catholicism, which institutionalizes the universalism of this new consciousness and then provides the context for its continuing development in the church.

Paul's role in all this is critical. For Paul the Judaizers (his opponents in Galatians) err because they wish to reintroduce into Christianity the element of particularity which Christianity as a religion of spirit had transcended. The positive side of this polemic, however, is his vision of Christian community: that 'all who are baptized into Christ enter at once, in that very act, into a new community, in which all the causes of division between man and man, which are to be found in the outward circumstances of life, are at once removed, so that there is no difference any longer between the Jew and the Greek, between circumcision and uncircumcision, but all may regard themselves as children of Abraham' (59f.).

Baur's theme is that in Christianity, specifically in Paul, a new self-consciousness comes to expression, which arises out of the new political and cultural constellation which is created by the emergence of the Roman principate and its hegemony over the Mediterranean world. The characteristics of this new mode of existence are the transcendence of particularity in favour of universalism, the supersession of the outward by the spiritual. Thus it is in the Pauline doctrine of life 'according to the Spirit' as opposed to the flesh that the centre of this new mode of universalizing self-consciousness is to be seen. To live such life in the Spirit is to be taken up into the mysteries of God; for the spiritual person 'has the mind of Christ' (I Cor. 2.16).

Thus on Baur's Hegelian view of history Christianity is the vehicle through which a new mode of human self-consciousness comes to expression. In that sense it is a new cultural phenomenon which comes to birth through a difficult dialectical process. Yet for all its newness it is not unrelated to the cultural and social developments of its time: it is rather the purest expression of such developments. Moreover the Christian conviction of having the mind of Christ brings with it an enormous sense of freedom, of transcending the finite and particular, which impels Christianity to reach out and transcend all cultural distinctions.

The problems with the details of Baur's interpretation of Paul are by now notorious. The history of religions school sought to show that Paul's language of the spirit owed more to the popular religion of the first century with its many ecstatic phenomena than to the philosophy of Spirit.[2] More recently, scholars such as W. D. Davies[3] and E. P. Sanders[4] have argued powerfully that Paul's thought is to be understood as arising out of a predominantly Jewish milieu. And others, notably Krister Stendahl[5] and Richard B. Hays,[6] have portrayed Paul as a theologian of salvation history, locating the saving events of the cross and resurrection within the wider biblical narrative of God's dealings with his people Israel. The picture of a universalizing, specifically non-particularizing, Paul, bringing to expression the new self-consciousness of the emerging empire, is now being replaced by a Jewish Paul who stresses the continuities between the new life in Christ and the history of God's dealings with his people the Jews – and yet in the process lays the basis for a profound split between Jews and Christians.

How far, then, can we now say that Pauline Christianity represents an attempt to construct a multicultural community? Certainly in so far as Paul saw himself called to be the apostle to the Gentiles and Pauline Christianity stood by the principle of opening the doors to Gentiles, it took on that challenge. It would have to face the problems of welding together people of different cultural traditions. The questions here are: does this movement draw on deep impulses within early Christianity, despite the obvious opposition which it encountered from some? Or: is it rather a reflection of the wider tendencies within the empire to cultural tolerance and diversity? And: what strategies did Christianity develop for undertaking such a task? How far did it draw on models which were already in existence?

1. Differences between intercultural relations in Paul's churches and the dominant pattern of cultural interchange in Greco-Roman cities

Ramsay Macmullen[7] has painted a vivid picture of the extraordinary cultural diversity of first century Greco-Roman cities. Cults from all over the Mediterranean would jostle alongside each other, inviting participation from all comers. Official tolerance of such cults was remarkably broad, always with the proviso that new cults did not wrap themselves in secrecy and that they respected and tolerated each other. Thus both Judaism and Christianity would from time to time fall under suspicion, partly because of the secrecy which surrounded Christian rites, partly because of their refusal to participate in other cults. In general, however, Judaism was respected, partly because of its antiquity, partly because of its high moral code.

The extent to which Christianity was willing to participate in such cultural diversity clearly varied among different groups and was most likely influenced by social position and experience. The *locus classicus* of this is in the discussion in I Corinthians of food offered to idols. It is clear that certain members of the congregation participated in meals in temples, where the food put before the diners would have been previously sacrificed to the god to whom the temple was dedicated. As such meals were relatively public, it would have been possible for other members of the congregation to have observed and been offended by such practices. In I Cor. 8, which seems to be directly addressed to those who accepted such invitations to dinner, Paul argues that the idols to which such food has been offered 'have no existence', but that rather than offend the conscience of the 'weak', the 'strong' should desist from eating meat. Indeed Paul gives a somewhat hedged undertaking not to eat meats himself. Much the same advice is given in I Cor. 10.27ff. which, however, contrasts rather surprisingly with the immediately preceding passage vv. 10–22, where Paul asserts that while food offered to idols is nothing, nevertheless it is offered to demons and that members of the congregation should not be partners with demons.

As G. Theissen has argued,[8] the difference between the 'strong' and the 'weak' is best understood in social terms: the 'strong' came from the wealthy stratum of society where attendance at such meals will have been necessary for social advancement and where the eating of meat will have been a relatively common occurrence. By contrast, the poor members of the congregation will have probably only had the opportunity to eat meat at pagan festivals and will have therefore tended to have much stronger religious feelings about it. While those with an assured position in society may have found it relatively easy to embrace Christianity without a total abandonment of their former life-style (adopting another oriental cult will not necessarily have attracted adverse attention), for those from the lower strata it may have meant more dramatic changes and caused a great sense of disorientation.

In sum: within Paul's churches there were some, probably largely from the upper stratum of society, who wished to continue associations with the culturally diverse life of the city. While Paul is clearly not wholly opposed to such associations, there were clearly also powerful forces within his churches which impelled them to break off any close association with the surrounding culture. On such a view the cultural groupings and activities of the Greco-Roman world have to be seen as part of the old dispensation from which Christians have been released. The new society into which all may be integrated is to be built on different foundations.

Paul's theological ambivalence in this case may also reflect something of his uncertainty about the appropriateness of Christian participation in the social and cultural life of the Greco-Roman city. Should he regard questions of participation in the cults as theological adiaphora, matters of indifference, or should he see this as a matter of faithfulness to the gospel: 'I do not want you to be partners with demons'? Certainly in Galatians, where his principal concern is with the reintroduction of the observation of the Law, he regards observation of pagan rituals as a return to bondage to beings that are no gods (Gal. 4.8). Moreover, in Thessalonica it appears that there was little opportunity for participation in the life of the wider community, even if the congregation had wished. They are sons of light, of the day, and not of the night and the darkness (I Thess. 5.5). If Acts (17.1–15) is to be believed, the congregation in Thessalonica was soon subject to discrimination and attack by the local Jewish community.

2. Theological motifs contributing to the subsuming of cultural differences into a new religious community

'For neither circumcision counts for anything, nor uncircumcision, but a new creation' (Gal. 6.15). J. L. Martyn[9] has argued that in Galatians Paul refers to a set of pairs of opposites: Jew/Greek, slave/free, male/female, which are to be transcended in the new world which is inaugurated by the crucifixion. Such sets of polar opposites are typical ways in the ancient world of signifying the very foundations of the world. The 'new creation' which Paul announces transcends such polarities, so that in baptism, Gal. 3.28, there is neither Jew nor Greek, there is neither slave nor free, there is neither male nor female; for you are all one in Christ Jesus. As Martyn writes: 'Perhaps in this final paragraph Paul is telling the Galatians that the whole of his epistle is . . . about the death of one world, and the advent of another' (414).

In the process of this new world's coming to be there are, however, set up new pairs of opposites (Martyn speaks of antinomies) which characterize the struggle between the new and the old age. Here instead of flesh (the 'evil impulse') being opposed by the Law, we find instead that flesh and Law are both opposed by the Spirit. These two realities are 'opposed orbs of power, actively at war with one another *since* the apocalyptic advent of Christ and of his Spirit. The space in which human beings now live is a newly invaded space, and that means that its structures cannot remain unchanged' (417).

On such a view, Paul's theology is counter-cultural. It sets out a view of the world according to which, *contrary to the appearances*, it is no longer evident socio-cultural distinctions which determine its true nature but rather an event in God's dealings with the world: the cross and resurrection of his Son. This requires a new way of looking at the world; and it inaugurates a new community where the old distinctions may be over-come. That is to say, on Paul's view he is not *building* a multicultural community at all. He is announcing the advent of a new community in Christ and issuing a call to people to enter it and to be reconciled. The claim is that this is in no way a reflection of cultural tendencies in the ancient world but the declaration of a new reality which relegates all existing culture to the old age which is passing away.

It is one thing to ask of Galatians what motivated it, what was the driving – cultural – force which led to Paul's letter; another to consider what place Paul himself envisaged for social and cultural divisions within his congregations. Paul's text in Gal. 3.28 is terse and gnomic. Did he look for the setting aside of all cultural differences in a new community which would be uniform in its cultural and social composition? One way of reading the text would indeed be to see it as outlawing distinctions such as those between Gentile and Jew, as having no place in the new world which is announced by the Gospel. On such a view those who wished to maintain their separate cultural identities would thereby show themselves to be incurably part of the old world and to have no place in the new, which is to be inhabited only by those who have been adopted as sons and daughters of God. Paul's anxiety about those among the Galatians who wish to observe the Law would go some way to reinforcing such a reading.

Or was Paul opposing any attempt to *absolutize* such distinctions, to see them as constitutive of the world *in such a manner that the boundaries between them had to be carefully upheld*? Paul is not opposing circumci-sion as such: what he is opposing is the contention that it is necessary for salvation and that it marks out the members of the – new – group from outsiders. In this respect his own practice is significant ('all things to all people', I Cor. 9.19–23), as is his doctrine of the justification of the ungodly. The God who inaugurates the new world is one who reaches out beyond the existing boundaries of Jew and Gentile to incorporate the enemy and the outcast (Rom. 5. 6,10). On such a view what is excluded is not particularity, not diversity *as such*, but cultural exclusivism, the absolutizing of cultural boundaries. The new creation is forged in an encounter with the stranger in which the old distinctions are subverted and new forms of life permitted to emerge. Moreover, as E. Käsemann has argued, such a view of justification is deeply christological.[10] The key, that is, lies in Paul's conviction that Christ died for the ungodly. The righteousness of God is a power that brings freedom and sonship to those who are weak, to those who are enemies, just as Jesus saw his mission being to the sick (Mark 2.17).[11]

3. Strategies for social integration in the new community

Baur was of course undisputably right to draw attention to the fact that Christianity came to birth during the Roman Principate, which represents the culmination of a long process of struggle by Rome to exercise effective control over the whole of the Mediterranean world. The success of this struggle required not only the military subjugation of powerful neighbours but the forging of social and political and economic structures which would ensure stability and peace. To this end Rome succeeded in integrating the patrician/democratic traditions of the cities into a military monarchy with overall control of military and fiscal policy. Political control was exercised not so much through a comprehensive administrative network cast over the area (as in the colonial administration of the British Empire) as through the control of key power points in the area: states and cities. Where their loyalty could be counted on without the imposition of direct rule, Rome was happy to allow a measure of local independence in return for financial and military support. In return for such loyalty, Rome provided overall protection and the benefits of good communications, peace and stability.

The creation of social cohesion in this vast new amalgam of societies was a task of major proportions. On the one hand a society which was sharply divided between upper and lower strata had to be held together; on the other regional units which were culturally diverse and with strong local rivalries had to learn to live in peace. A remarkable degree of integration was achieved partly through the continuance of existing local patterns of association in polis and state and partly through the establishment of supraregional loyalties to Caesar, in which the Emperor cult will have played no small part. Interestingly, it was the Jews who were most resistant to such integration, as the three major risings in the first two centuries CE demonstrate.

The church faced similar problems of integration, if on an altogether smaller scale. Christians were drawn largely from the lower strata of society, but also included members with larger houses and slaves. Christians included Jews and Gentiles and were scattered across the Mediterranean. They had some kind of a centre in Jerusalem, with a leadership which attempted to exercise some overall control, but such attempts at interference were resisted and resented by charismatic figures such as Paul.

As G. Theissen has suggested,[12] the ways in which the early Christian communities attempted to maintain their unity reflect patterns of social integration in the Principate. The personal bond between the Emperor and his subjects which helped to maintain supraregional unity can be compared with that between Christ and the believer; early christology uses terms to be found also in the Emperor cult: *kyrios, soter*, Son of God. Like the Emperor, Christ brings peace (though not of this world, John 14.27) and integrates both Jews and Gentiles into a world-wide community (Eph. 2.1ff.); the message of such benefits is in both cases referred to as *euaggelion*. Just as citizens and cities might transcend their local rivalries in virtue of their bond to Caesar, so Christians could find a new unity with one another which transcended cultural differences in their charismatic relationship to the Lord.

One might add that while such ways of constructing an overall sense of unity were predominant within Paul's churches, they were not the only ones. Alongside these have to be placed attempts to create a sense of allegiance to the 'pillars' in Jerusalem (Gal. 2.9) and in particular to James the brother of the Lord, and of course Paul's own attempts in his letters and journeys to secure the personal loyalty of 'his' churches to himself as father. Moreover Paul ties such loyalty into his own loyalty to the Lord in his plea to his churches to imitate him, as he is an imitator of Christ/the Lord (I Cor. 11.1; I Thess. 1.6).

Christians also had to face the same problems of integration locally that confronted the citizens of the Greco-Roman cities. Theoretically all members of the polis were equal: in practice there were huge discrepancies in wealth, social status and legal rights between wealthy citizens and members of the lower classes, including slaves, and between citizens and resident aliens, and between women and men. Christian communities in the cities around the Mediterranean will have had to deal with such inequalities too. Paul declares the fundamental equality of all, and in Gal. 3.28 specifically mentions those groups which would have been most disadvantaged in such cities: Jews, slaves and women. At the same time his letters testify to the need for the wealthy in the community to support the weaker members. The Letter to Philemon in which Paul appeals to the owner of a runaway slave to exercise Christian compassion to a brother gives an example of the way in which notions of the Christian family are employed to overcome the sharp social divisions which threatened its unity. In this way the social implications of the believer's charismatic relationship to his Lord are drawn out in terms of familial and social metaphors.

Conclusion

Early Christianity is beyond doubt a product of the cosmopolitan world of the first century. It is not, however, simply a reflection of the culture of the Roman Principate. In some respects its ethos is profoundly counter-cultural, announcing a new creation which is already present, by contrast with which the present age is merely a world of appearances which is passing away. In this respect it relativizes the major cultural divisions of its time and seeks to overcome social barriers and boundaries in the name of a Lord who comes to save the lost, the weak and the enemies of God. At the same time it is receptive to integrating or universalizing tendencies within the culture and responsive to its internal tensions. In its attempts to secure social integration within its own membership early Christianity explores possibilities of association which will be realized, in part at least, when it gains recognition under Constantine.

Notes

1. References to the third English edition, London 1787–9.
2. See my *A Century of New Testament Study*, Cambridge 1993, 31–49.
3. *Paul and Rabbinic Judaism*, London 1948.
4. *Paul and Palestinian Judaism*, London 1977
5. *Paul among Jews and Gentiles*, Philadelphia 1976.
6. *Echoes of Scripture in the Letters of Paul*, New Haven 1989.
7. *Paganism in the Roman Empire*, New Haven 1981.
8. 'The Strong and the Weak in Corinth: A Sociological Analysis of Theological Quarrel', in *The Social Setting of Pauline Christianity*, Edinburgh 1982, 121–43.
9. 'Apocalyptic Antinomies in Paul's Letter to the Galatians', *New Testament Studies* 31, 1985, 410–24.
10. *Commentary on Romans*, London 1980, 24.
11. Ibid., 317.
12. 'Some Ideas about a Sociological Theory of Early Christianity', in *Social Reality and the Early Christians*, Minneapolis 1992, 272ff.

II · From Scroll to World: The Bible and the Making of Culture

The Bible in Arts and Literature: Source of Inspiration for Poets and Painters

Mary Magdalen

David Jasper

In his book *The Implied Reader* (1974), Wolfgang Iser lays stress on the extent to which the 'unwritten' part of a text stimulates reading and creative response. What is *not* there is as important as what is there in the text, the literary work realized in the reading which brings together text and reader. Any text is 'virtual' – full of gaps and omissions which the busily imaginative reading process repairs and completes.[1] The coherence which may be apparent at the conclusion of this process in fact will inevitably be a construction resulting not least from the disposition and predilections of the reader or a group of readers.

Readings against the grain of accepted or common interpretations will tend to expose what Mieke Bal has called the 'gaps, breaks, inconsistencies, and problems' which underlie ideologically or theologically driven readings of texts, and, she suggests, it is precisely these gaps which are finally more interesting than the smoothly cemented, systematic structures.[2] As a feminist critic, Bal is particularly concerned with those fractures which occur with respect to figures who are outside the primary interest of a church and its ideology, these being, all too often, women as marginalized through particular perceptions of gender. Elisabeth Schüssler Fiorenza makes a similar point in her book *In Memory of Her*, referring to the figure of Mary Magdalen:

How much scriptural interpretation and legitimization served political functions for the church can be illustrated by the example of Mary of Magdala.[3]

Mary's identity does not emerge coherently from the texts of the four Gospels. The contexts in which she is named, and particularly Mark 16.9 and John 20.10–18, tend to fall into the background of the legends of Mary as the penitent whore (Luke 7; John 8), the contemplative sister of Martha and Lazarus (John 11), and, linked by John 11.2, the woman who anoints Jesus' feet and wipes them with her hair (Matthew 26; Mark 14; John 12). It is possible to see how connections between these apparently quite distinct women might have been made – in Mark 16.9 (almost certainly a later addition to the original Gospel which finishes at 16.8), the description of Mary as one 'from whom [Jesus] had formerly cast out seven devils' could link her with the repentant prostitute of Luke 7. What seems clear is, first, how quickly these identifications began to be made, and second, the function of this process in the politics of the early church.

For example, it seems odd that in the Johannine version of the first announcement of the resurrection, Mary of Magdala tells the disciples of her encounter with Jesus in the garden (John 20.18), and there is no hint that she was disbelieved. In both Mark and Luke, however, the suggestion that they did not believe her story is present in verses which have a debatable place in the text (Mark 16.9–12; Luke 24.12), and are frequently omitted because they are regarded as later additions. In Luke's version, Peter actually goes to check up and see for himself, suggesting an early development in Christian thinking that, first, a male witness alone is reliable, and, second, it should be the witness of Peter to whom the church looks back as its 'rock'. In Gnostic literature such as the *Gospel of Philip* and the *Gospel of Mary* there is open rivalry between Mary Magdalen and the male disciples, the Gnostic tradition favouring Mary's witness, while increasingly the literature of orthodox communities such as the *Apostolic Church Order* of the late second century marginalizes Mary on the basis of her previously questionable status. Here John says to Mary, 'Your weakness is redeemed through strength',[4] with the clear implication that one should never really trust a woman like this. The early church, it seems, finds it necessary to construct the figure of Mary Magdalen from the brief suggestion of Mark 16.9 in order to establish and legitimate its patriarchal notions of apostolicity.

Furthermore, Marina Warner suggests that it was necessary to promote the composite identity of Mary Magdalen from the disparate women in the Gospels in order to complement the inalienable virginity of the other

Mary, the mother of Jesus. Together these two Marys typify the church's attitudes to women and sex.

> Both female figures are perceived in sexual terms: Mary as a virgin and Mary Magdalene as a whore – until her repentance. The Magdalene, like Eve, was brought into existence by the powerful undertow of misogyny in Christianity, which associates women with the dangers and degradations of the flesh.[5]

There is, therefore, a powerful politics of coherence working to bring together fragmentary scriptural references to create a role for Mary Magdalen which cements the obvious gaps and inconsistencies in the texts, and that politics is at work from the very earliest stages of development in the debateable verses of Mark and Luke,

The story, however, is more complex still. For in the earliest Christian art, Mary remains prominent as the *Apostola Apostolorum*, appearing, for example, in the early third-century frescoes at Dura-Europos. This imagery which places emphasis on the act of witness by Mary and the other women is repeated frequently in art. Significantly, Hippolytus, Bishop of Rome (c. 170–235 CE), almost contemporary with the Dura-Europos paintings, while being the first to grant to Mary Magdalen the title of 'Apostle to the Apostles', theologizes her persona by associating her through the Bride of the Song of Songs with the Bride of Christ and symbol of the church – titles more often associated with the Virgin Mary.[6]

Theology, it appears, has always felt the need to overcome its embarrassment at that moment in the garden when Mary, perhaps even after Peter and the other disciple 'whom Jesus loved' had entered the empty tomb (John 20.1–9), alone sees the Lord and, recognizing him in his resurrected form, on his instruction first announces his appearance. The powerful sexuality and even scandal of that moment is dispersed by the cynicism of male response (Mark 16.11; Luke 24.11) and its reappropriation into the more useful legend of Mary as the repentant whore and the *beata peccatrix*, whose very touch might pollute the resurrected flesh of her Lord. Thus, Thomas Aquinas openly suggests that 'it seems . . . that there was a certain unfittingness in the fact that Christ appeared after his resurrection first to women, and then to the others'. He goes on to remark that Christ's refusal to allow Mary to touch him, the *'noli me tangere'*, is the result of the fear of pollution in contrast to his subsequent invitation to Thomas (whose doubt and hesitancy become almost a virtue after Mary's readiness to embrace Jesus and eagerness to believe) to touch his wounds. In the extraordinary painting of 'Doubting Thomas' attributed to Caravaggio, now in Potsdam, Thomas's fingers actually intrude into Jesus' side. Earlier in mediaeval art these two moments of Mary and Thomas in the Fourth Gospel are frequently juxtaposed to underscore the two different types of witness.[7]

Art and literature concerning Mary Magdalen, I suggest, both sustain the constructed narratives of church and tradition and, at the same time, disrupt and deconstruct them. Early Gnostic descriptions of the hostility of Peter towards Mary repeatedly indicate the sexual element in the relationship between Jesus and Mary which the identification of Mary with the penitent whore in Luke 7 serves to elide and deal with. The *Gospel of Philip* affirms that

> . . . the companion of the [Saviour is] Mary Magdalen. [But Christ loved] her more than [all] the disciples and used to kiss her [often] on her [mouth]. The rest of [the disciples were offended by it . . .]
>
> They said to him, 'Why do you love her more than all of us?' The Saviour answered and said to them, 'Why do I not love you as [I love] her?'[8]

Michèle Roberts' novel *The Wild Girl* (1984) sustains this sexual theme as a 'narrative novel' which Roberts overtly constructs in the tradition of the Gospels ('Author's Note'), suggesting that 'a narrative novel creates a myth in the same way [as the Gospels]: I wanted to dissect a myth; I found myself at the same time recreating one.'

Literature about Mary Magdalen repeatedly tends to lean towards the Gnostic affirmation of Mary as witness and, by extension, one who enjoys a particular relationship with Jesus. John Donne in his sonnet 'To Mrs Magdalen Herbert: of St Mary Magdalen' affirms that

> An active faith so highly did advance,
>   That she once knew, more than the Church did know,
> The Resurrection.

Part of this 'knowledge' is seemingly ineradicably preserved in paintings of the so-called Conversion of Mary Magdalen, a subject created to accompany her role as a converted sinner. In Caravaggio's version (c. 1600), now in Detroit, Mary is magnificently dressed in a revealing gown, being advised by the figure of Martha to her right. Symbolically on the table in front of her is a damaged comb and a cosmetic bowl with a sponge, now rejected. Holding an orange blossom to her heart with her right hand, her left hand rests on a mirror – symbol both of vanity and truth – which reflects a brilliant square of light from the window opposite. In her moment of conversion, Mary remains dazzlingly beautiful, even alluring, repentant yet profoundly sexual. A slightly later painting of the Penitent Magdalen by Artemesia Gentileschi similarly portrays her in a sumptuous, low-cut gown, her left hand rejecting the jewels, her right hand clasped to her heart at the moment of conversion – or else clasping her semi-revealed breast. It has been suggested that the gold of her dress relates to the liturgical colour of her feast day – but each symbol can be read ambiguously. To the artist, Mary's sexuality remains as part of her conversion – a moment of artistic voyeurism, or perhaps the enduring presence of something more profound which the church and its theology would obliterate. Even the saintly poet George Herbert preserves something of this presence in his poem 'Marie Magdalene':

When blessed Marie wip'd her Saviors feet,
    (Whose precepts she had trampled on before)
And wore them for a jewell on her head . . .

In repentance Mary remains adorned, as one of her biblical personae wipes her Master's feet with her hair.

Both the poetry and the art fragment the composite narrative which the church and its politics makes for Mary Magdalen, catching moments which expose her troubling complexity even as they illustrate the theology. Both theology and art have, in Leo Steinberg's word, their oblivions,[9] their protections against 'life', although, I would argue, art and literature have an immediacy which renders more apparent the 'inconsistencies, and problems that any ideology necessarily entails'.[10] Even art acts to repress the delegitimate immediate responses, especially sexual, by its formal languages of interpretation and response. But still the images demand our attention and our gaze at a primary, pre-rational stage.

We talk about colours and form. If we suspect arousal we deny it or – at best and most liberated – are mildly ashamed. This may be the pure paradox of looking, but there is – as so often – a further paradox. We have, clearly, to look more closely at the ways and implications of repression; but at the same time we realize fully the possibility that there is no arousal without repression.[11]

We turn now to that central and most complex moment in the scriptural history of Mary Magdalen, her encounter in the garden with Jesus in John 20.

Here, above all, the subject is the resurrection body. St Augustine in the *City of God* (413–26 CE) describes the perfection of the resurrected body in great detail (Book XXII, 14–15), likening all those resurrected to the resurrected Christ, even to the same age ('about thirty years'). Augustine specifically addresses the question 'will women retain their sex in the resurrected body' (Ch. 17), and concludes that women who remain virgins can 'become male' by cultivating the male prerogatives of spirituality and rationality.[12] Although Augustine concludes that male and female bodies will be maintained in resurrection, he sustains a specifically male image of beauty and reduces the *functions* of the female body to a male spirituality, *concupiscentia* (sexual lust) being specifically identified with female sexuality. In other words, gender difference is, according to Augustine, overcome in the perfect, resurrected condition, normativity being attributed to the male.

Despite notable exceptions such as Signorelli's briefly influential *Resurrection of the Flesh*, painted in the Chapel of the Madonna of San Brizio in Orvieto – with its beautiful, clearly gendered bodies, initially so influential upon Michelangelo in his Sistine Last Judgment, painted forty years later in 1541 – the history of Christian art has been deeply influenced by Augustine's thinking on the body. Suspicion of the human body and its fleshly potential found acute expression when, in December 1563, the Council of Trent banned 'unsuitable subjects' from religious images, an order immediately interpreted as meaning nudity. Michelangelo's naked figures were clothed, first by one of his own pupils, and then successively in 1572, 1625, 1712 and 1762.

Signorelli's painting affirms gender difference in the resurrected flesh, perfect male and perfect female, while not acknowledging what the biologist Ruth Hubbard has characterized as 'gender socialization'.[13] In other words Signorelli's women match his men in size, expressiveness and muscularity. But, to return to the garden, where a resurrected body is first perceived – that of the male Christ himself – the tradition in art of the '*noli me tangere*' (John 20.17) is clearly stylized. In Titian's painting in the National Gallery, for example, we see the city in the distance, the tree – reminiscent of the earlier garden, Eden – and Mary, in her scarlet robe, kneeling in an attitude of supplication before a Jesus who, by any standards, can hardly be mistaken for a gardener. Wielding a spindly little hoe, he is dressed more or less in a loincloth reminiscent of his crucifixion, and is backing away from Mary's extended hand. The angels of John 20.12 are nowhere in evidence. Titian is clearly following the 'narrativized theology'[14] of the church which encloses Mary in the legend of the repentant prostitute and denies her a 'voice' in the encounter with Jesus. The archetypical 'fallen woman', with long fair hair, she kneels before the resurrected one whom she may not touch.

This theological justification of Jesus is sustained in the 'orthodox' tradition of reading John 20. Thus, in the mid-nineteenth century a number of journals appeared concerned to reclaim 'fallen women' or 'Magdalens', one, 'edited by a clergyman, and devoted to the cause of the Fallen', entitled *Magdalen's Friend and Female Homes' Intelligencer* carrying in its 'Monthly Address' in 1860 the following:

> 'Woman, why weepest thou?' . . . [These words] were spoken by Jesus, the son of God, after His resurrection, to Mary Magdalen, a poor sinner, whom He found weeping beside His tomb. What He says to her, He says to you, 'Woman, why weepest thou?' Her sins which had been many, were forgiven, and Jesus, her Saviour, condescends now to notice and enquire into the cause of her grief. He whom she had pierced by her sins is now concerned at the sight of her sorrow . . . Will you not, like Mary of old, fall upon your knees before Him, and seek but to touch the hem of His garment that you may be whole?[15]

And so the construct of Mary continues – but at the same time the Gospel text itself provokes other possibilities and complexities. Commentators on John 20.1–18 frequently refer to awkwardnesses in the text[16] which suggest that in fact a number of independent episodes are brought together here. In particular there is the odd moment when the angels, unlike their counterparts in other Gospels, merely interrogate Mary without offering her comfort or reassurance. Why did Mary see angels, particularly such unhelpful ones, when the two male disciples see nothing but an empty tomb? And what does the prohibition to touch in v. 17 really imply? For a moment that becomes so important in theology and art that this is textually very unclear as to its precise meaning. One commentator even suggests that it may amount to little more than 'fear not'.[17]

Given the frequent connection made between Mary Magdalen and Eve – she being the one who repents of Eve's 'sin' – it is perhaps not altogether surprising that art introduces into this already textually unstable passage a reference to the earlier garden of Eden. John Ruskin in *Sesame and Lilies* (1865) wrote:

> Did you ever hear, not of a Maud, but a Madeleine, who went down into her garden in the dawn, and found one waiting at the gate, whom she supposed to be the gardener? Have you not sought Him often; – sought Him in vain, all through the night; – sought Him in vain at the gate of that old garden where the fiery sword is set? He is never there; but at the gate of *this* garden He is waiting always – waiting to take your hand . . .

Mary's Easter garden here becomes the antithesis of the Eden from which Adam and Eve have been evicted, guarded by the cherubim with fiery sword (Gen. 3.14). Where theological construction has endeavoured to smooth interpretation, a text already pitted with inconsistencies and evidences of editorial weavings continues to prompt complex typological references and imaginative expansion. And so we come to the extraordinary painting by Rembrandt, dated 1638, now in Buckingham Palace.

If Titian's 'Noli Me Tangere' demands to be read through a long theological tradition which has filtered the images of the Johannine text, Rembrandt's painting keeps us worryingly on the complex surface of its text and reopens the primary fissures of the Gospel, demanding a changed perspective of the viewer. For Mary Magdalen here is released from the conventions of her legend as a loving, penitent whore. Titian primarily focuses upon the figure of the risen Jesus: Rembrandt is concerned to explore the dilemma of Mary herself. In many respects the painting is conventional – the city in the background, the tree with even a hint of a snake, even Mary's red gown. But this is not the moment of v. 17, the *'noli me tangere'*. In fact the picture itself is a kind of narrative, almost deconstructing the narratives of orthodox theological readings. The central figures of the picture – Jesus, Mary and the two angels – enact v. 14. With these words she turned round and saw Jesus standing there, but did not recognize him. But there are two other figures in the picture – to the far left, they appear to be walking away while *one* of them looks backwards to what is centrally going on. One must assume that these are Peter and the 'one whom Jesus loved', who, in verse 10 'went home again' . . . (an odd phrase in Greek).[18] In other words, Rembrandt's painting is telling the story of John 20.10–14/15.

My first question concerns the two retreating figures. Although there is no evidence in the Gospel to suggest this, it appears as though at least one of them is well aware of Mary's encounter with angels and Jesus (though presumably no one recognizes him at this stage), and is prepared to leave her to fend for herself. The male disciples, it seems, prefer to get away as quickly as possible, rendering problematical the later tradition which claims Peter rather than Mary as the primary witness for the resurrection. John 20.8–9 affirms that these two disciples already 'believed' by this time on the evidence of the empty tomb. Are they then here getting away from what could be construed as a rather nasty encounter for a lone woman?

Jesus, unlike Titian's ethereal figure, here is dashing, almost a bandit. Wearing a broad-brimmed hat and wielding a fairly serviceable-looking spade, he also sports a rather menacing curved knife in his belt. By his posture he might well be a local coming around the corner of the rock to see what is going on. His gaze is directed solely towards Mary, despite the clear presence of two angels, white robes, wings and all.

The Gospel never suggests that anyone saw the angels apart from Mary.

Nor does Rembrandt's painting. The single male figure, if one did not know the context, could be menacing, indeed is apparently taken by Mary to be so, given her terrified expression and attitude. Mary herself has many conventional details of her character in the tradition. Her scarlet gown is worn over seemingly rich garments in her role as repentant prostitute. Beside her on the ground is a jar and other objects presumably linked to the task of anointing the body – although this purpose for visiting the tomb is never mentioned in the Fourth Gospel. But her central position in the picture has a complexity which is far beyond the conventional. One of the angels has a hand extended as if he is speaking, suggesting that this is precisely the moment of the angelic conversation with Mary (v. 13). Mary turns her face even while her hand is outstretched towards her angelic interlocutor, startled by the appearance of the strange man behind her who seems to be entirely oblivious of the angels. Mary's mood is fearful and confused. Seemingly this is the moment before she concludes that this must be the gardener and recovers the power of speech. It is utterly different from the beseeching adoration of Titian's 'Noli Me Tangere' or the tradition which has Jesus comforting the weeping Mary, the figure who 'condescends to notice and enquire into the cause of her grief'. The immediate sense of this painting, before the conventions of the theological narrative begin to obscure its gaps and problems, is one of distraction and fear with clear undercurrents of sexual threat, while the male disciples (not for the first time) get out of the way when they see things turning potentially nasty.

None of this would deny a resolution in the next few moments which is entirely benign. But Rembrandt, I suggest, has framed a moment of utter panic which could go either way. Both angels and men are at best unhelpful, and there is a powerful, unresolved chemistry between herself and a strange, armed man. The undertones of brutality can be extended in the biblical text to v. 17, by which time Mary has established the identity of the man as her beloved Master, who yet refuses to grant her physical contact.[19] In the spirit of Rembrandt's picture, her impulse to hold him may be simply the quite natural one of relief when she realizes that the man who had frightened her is in fact a friend, and, indeed, more than just a friend.

I recognize, of course, that this reading of Rembrandt's painting is tending to construct conjectural narratives against the spirit of traditional scriptural interpretation and legitimization. But that is precisely my point. For, given that critics agree that John 20.1–18 is a difficult and probably multi-layered text, it is part of a fragmented and highly conjectural theological tradition which has constructed the composite figure of Mary

Magdalen out of disparate bits and pieces in order to grant her a role in its patriarchal religion and ideology. The church and its legends, in other words, have 'used' the text conjecturally for their own purposes, and art and literature repeatedly present seepages of elements in the story which tend to work against these traditional 'narratives', and invite other conjectural readings.

In Rembrandt, I suggest, there is a strong sexual element which discomforts the control of sexuality exercised by the notion of Mary as the repentant sinner, as the 'Magdalen' or restored 'fallen woman'. The chemistry of threat between the man and the woman may be developed into a more explicit eroticism (already present in Hippolytus of Rome's typological use of the Song of Songs to related Jesus and Mary Magdalen), as in Eric Gill's 1922 engraving *The Nuptials of God* in the Victoria and Albert Museum, of Christ on the cross entirely covered by Mary, her outstretched arms covering his, nailed to the cross, her evident nakedness concealed by her long hair,[20] the two heads clearly met in a loving kiss. Both figures are surmounted by haloes. Gill is attracted by the ancient notion of Mary Magdalen as symbol of the church and bride of Christ, combining his adopted Roman Catholicism with an overt eroticism which shocked the Catholic church. In art the sexual communication between Jesus and Mary Magdalen seems inescapable even, or perhaps especially, when religious motivation seeks to divert or repress it.

In literature, D. H. Lawrence's rather heavy-handed story 'The Man Who Died' (1929) emphasizes the theme of sexuality, and if the 'Madeleine' whom the unnamed man/Jesus meets in the garden is rejected in so far as she maintains her traditional role of the repentant sinner, the later sexual encounter with the mythic Isis (with whom, in some Gnostic sects, Mary Magdalen seem to have been linked[21]) is clearly intended to be related to Mary as the goddess anoints the man's wounds (cf. Mark 16.1; Luke 23.56) and appears dressed like 'Madeleine'. Here, as in Eric Gill's engraving, Mary Magdalen's sexuality, far from being repressed and repented of, actually becomes the instrument of 'the man's' salvation. Nikos Kazantzakis in *Report to Greco* (1961) develops the theme, Mary possessing the life-giving power actually to resurrect Christ. Kazantzakis combines this with her ancient connection with the Song of Songs, Mary dreaming of the Rabbi, enticing him in her dreams.

> See, as a bride I dress and preen.
> My palms and soles I paint with henna, my eyes
> with dilute kohl, and a beauty spot joins my brows.
> . . . And when by flowering

paths I finally reach your beloved tomb,
like a woman, Christ, forsaken by her lover,
may you leave me . . . I shall talk, and clasp
your pallid knees . . . Though all deny you, Christ,
you will not die, for in my breast I hold
the immortal water; I give it to you, and upon the
earth you mount once more and walk with me
in the meadows.[22]

Kazantzakis' poem combines a number of disparate scriptural references, centring upon the image in Titian's painting, only in Kazantzakis the kneeling woman both touches and offers Christ fulfilment in sexual union.

By contrast, Kazantzakis' more notorious *The Last Temptation* (1959), proscribed by the Vatican and the subject of vicious vilification by many Christian churches following Martin Scorsese's film of the book, takes the ultimately more 'orthodox' line of Christ rejecting the temptations of the flesh, personified by Mary Magdalen. In the novel it is Jesus who, by initially rejecting Mary's sexuality, drives her to a life of prostitution before he rescues her from stoning by Barabbas the Zealot and she becomes his devoted follower. Jesus' final temptation on the cross is a vision of domestic bliss with Mary Magdalen as Woman – the universal symbol of man's temptation to abandon God. Kazantzakis' Mary Magdalen is, like the Mary of Christian tradition, a composite figure from scripture. Precisely that complexity allows space for a hermeneutics of suspicion, that is, a shifting in perspective which redefines the elements, and their power, in Mary's character and situation. If the church has insistently regarded the woman in the garden as the figure of the repentant sinner, and the one who anoints Jesus' feet and wipes them with her hair, art and literature, even where it follows this tradition of the church, has always been edgy and tended to ruffle the smooth surface of the theological narrative. The latent cruelty of John 20.17, however justified it might be theologically, repeatedly surfaces, as for example in Michèle Roberts' novel *The Wild Girl* (1984), where Mary reacts not with unquestioning obedience, as in the Johannine narrative, but with mixed feelings.

I did not want to hear him say it. My joy at seeing him was mixed with sharp pain, as had so often been the case in the weeks before his death, when I embraced him and tasted the sweetness of his mouth and felt his arms around me and at the same time feared for him, feared for his safety, for the moment when the soldiers would come and take him away. I looked at his face, which was always beautiful to me, and prayed for the courage to accept the truth he offered me.[23]

As I draw towards a conclusion, I return to Rembrandt's great painting. It is by no means the only time he painted this encounter between Jesus and Mary Magdalen. Much more conventionally there is Rembrandt's 'Noli Me Tangere', painted in 1651 and now in Brunswick. This is close in spirit to the Titian of John 20.17, except that the figure of Jesus is more ethereal, a halo of light shining from his head and with not even a token sign that he might be taken for a gardener. Rembrandt's risen Lord, his right hand raised in blessing, even here seems barely in the flesh. Mary kneels in a conventional posture of devotion.

More interesting is a sketch of 1638, which has been suggested as a preparatory note for the great painting of the same year. It portrays the instant after the moment of the painting, the moment of Jesus' question, John 20.15. In the far distance again we see the two retreating figures of the disciples. Beside Mary is her jar, she having recovered from her initial fright and fallen down upon her knees. Jesus, again in broad-brimmed hat and with spade, is leaning nonchalantly with his right arm on a ledge, looking down on the woman. In this instant what might be surmised, given Jesus' question: 'Why are you weeping? Who is it you are looking for?'? Given that Mary still has not recognized him, and takes him at best to be a gardener, from her point of view this is hardly a pleasant situation. Frightened and confused, alone, with a strange man interrogating her, in Rembrandt's drawing adopting a potentially threatening pose, *out of the familiar context of the justifying theological narrative* this is a charged and uncomfortable moment. It could have many outcomes.

My purpose in this article is not, finally, to deny readings of John 20.1–18 within the Christian tradition. It is, however, simply to expose the conventionality and arbitrariness of such readings as they create a composite figure from textually discrete elements in the Gospels and shape the material to particular purposes, for example, the tendency to ensure that male disciples and not Mary of Magdala become the primary witnesses of the resurrection. Phenomenologically, as Wolfgang Iser would insist, this shaping in the reading process goes on all the time in all reading, as 'reader and author participate in a game of the imagination'.[24] Art and literature, in representing a narrative or an image, may do so entirely in the service of the theological configurations of church and tradition. Fine poems such as Richard Crashaw's 'Saint Mary Magdalene; or, the Weeper' or Robert Southwell's 'Mary Magdalen's Blush' emerged directly out of Counter-Reformation piety using the themes and images of the legend. But, at the same time, the artistic imagination will tend to shake loose from the strict demands of 'orthodoxy', consciously or unconsciously, with an almost inevitable degree of anxiety. Images and motifs will take on a life of their own independently of the narrative demands of institution, and the eye of the poet or artist will seek new perspectives and new instances of engagement which offer new complexions to the story.

Thus we see Mary Magdalen not as the weeper, the penitent whore, the patient, forgiven woman, but the frightened, lonely figure in the garden, the lover denied a touch of the beloved (while Thomas, in his doubt, is invited to feel the wounds), or the woman whose vibrant sexuality, far from suffering pious repression, actually participates in the resurrection of her Lord. Above all, we see the ambiguous fearful moment of Rembrandt's painting: how does a Christian reading of John 20 absorb the human complexities of this artistic instant? Does it not precisely illustrate Mieke Bal's point that under such perspectives 'it is not so much the overall ideology that will come to the fore, but rather the gaps, breaks, inconsistencies and problems that any ideology necessarily entails'?[25]

In more ways than one we might say of Mary of Magdala, whoever she was, with the poet John Donne 'that she once knew, more that the Church did know' – and art continues to suggest that this is so.

Notes

1. Wolfgang Iser, *The Implied Reader*. Baltimore 1974, 174–94.

2. Mieke Bal, *Death and Dissymetry: The Politics of Coherence in the Book of Judges*, Chicago 1988, 34.

3. Elisabeth Schüssler Fiorenza, *In Memory of Her*. London and New York 1983, 304.

4. See Elaine Pagels, *The Gnostic Gospels*, Harmondsworth 1990, 84–5; Marina Warner, *Alone of All Her Sex*, London 1990, 224–35.

5. Warner, *Alone of All Her Sex* (n. 4), 225.

6. See Susan Haskins, *Mary Magdalen*, London 1993, 58–67.

7. Ibid. 178–9.

8. *Gospel of Philip* 63.32–64.5 in *The Nag Hammadi Library*, New York 1977, 138.

9. Leo Steinberg, *The Sexuality of Christ in Renaissance Art and Modern Oblivion*, New York 1983.

10. Bal, *Death and Dissymetry* (n. 2), 34.

11. David Freedberg, *The Power of Images*, Chicago and London 1989, 330.

12. See Margaret R. Miles, 'The Revelatory Body: Signorelli's *Resurrection of the Flesh* at Orvieto', *Arts: The Arts in Religious and Theological Studies* 6.1, 1993, 14–23.

13. Ruth Hubbard, 'Constructing Sex Difference', *New Literary History* 19.1, Autumn 1987, 131.

14. See Alison Jasper, 'Interpretative Approaches to John 20: 1–18. Mary at the Tomb of Jesus', *Studia Theologica* 47, 1993, 107–18.

15. *The Magdalen's Friend and Female Homes' Intelligencer* 1, 1860, 33.

16. For example: Raymond E. Brown, *The Gospel According to John*, Vol.II, Anchor Bible, New York, 1979, v. 11; C. K. Barrett, *The Gospel According to St John*, London 1955, v. 17; John Marsh, *Saint John*, Harmondsworth 1968, v. 17.

17. Barrett, *Gospel According to St John* (n. 16), 470.

18. Ibid., 469.

19. See Jasper, 'Interpretative Approaches' (n. 14), 112: ' . . . in terms of this as a narrative about Mary and not as it were, narrativized theology, Jesus' rejection or exclusion of Mary from the physical contact to which the text itself bears witness as her desire and intention, carries undertones of decided brutality which cannot be smoothed away.'

20. There is an ancient tradition that Mary ended her days as an ascetic in the desert, clothed only in her own hair, yet innocent and sexless, e.g. the panels by Quetin Metsys (1466–1530) of Mary Magdalen facing Mary of Egypt, both entirely naked except for long tresses, in attitudes of devout prayer, Philadelphia Museum of Art, John G. Johnson Collection.

21. See Haskins, *Mary Magdalen* (n. 6), 45.

22. Nikos Kazantzakis, *Report to Greco*, London 1973, 241–2.

23. Michèle Roberts, *The Wild Girl*, London 1991, 104–5.

24. Iser, *The Implied Reader* (n. 1), 275.

25. Bal, *Death and Dissymetry* (n. 2), 34.

The Bible and the Discovery of the World: Mission, Colonization and Foreign Development

Arnulf Camps

Many scholarly books and articles appeared in 1992 as part of the commemoration of the five hundredth anniversary of Columbus' landing on what is now called Latin America. An evaluation of this extensive literature leads to two conclusions. In the first place we can note that many authors have seen that it is of supreme importance to take the abundant sources from this period as a starting point for investigations: the sources are not only those which give us an insight into the political, religious, economic and cultural situation on the Iberian peninsula but also those which describe events in the New World both from the side of the conquerors and from the side of the conquered. And indeed around 1992 many such sources were edited or re-edited. The second conclusion relates to the use of these sources. Not all authors have seemed to be in a position to master the sources present on both sides. It is possible to put the emphasis one-sidedly on the Iberian background and underestimate the significance of events in Latin America. It is also possible to fail to do justice to the complicated and ambiguous mentality, above all of those who took part in the so-called spiritual conquest, by a one-sided interpretation of the sources which recorded events in the New World.

The aim of this article is to investigate the complicated and even ambiguous mentality of three important people who played a major role in the spiritual conquest. These are Christopher Columbus (1451–1506), Bartolomé de Las Casas OP (1474–1566), and Bernardino de Sahagún OFM (1499–1590). Our question is: what role did the Bible play in their attempt to justify as Christians their participation in the spiritual conquest of Latin America? All three were committed Christians and highly educated Westerners who played three different but leading roles during the first century of the conquest (1492–1590).

Our question can be briefly entitled 'Bible and Conquest'. Here the word conquest is understood in broad terms as covering both the secular and the spiritual conquest. Even then, colonization, mission and foreign influence went hand in hand; or, to put it in another way, these aspects are interwoven. The investigation of the three great personalities mentioned above is therefore of paradigmatic significance. And the investigation of the role of the Bible in all this is also paradigmatic; scripture is more than text and has always had to do with the human activity of seeking meaning in events and experiences which go beyond the individual and thus have a transcendent depth.[1]

1. Christopher Columbus and the prophecies

Columbus undertook four voyages with the aim of reaching Asia directly by a Western route (the Atlantic Ocean: 1492–1493; 1493–1496; 1498–1500; 1502–1503). He visited various islands lying off the continent of America and even lay off some of the coasts of that continent, but he never knew that he had not reached Asia but America. Columbus prepared himself thoroughly for his voyages. He investigated all the facts from antiquity, from the Bible, from mediaeval travellers to Asia, from theological and secular writings from previous centuries and from Portuguese explorers of the coasts of Africa. From this information he inferred that it must be possible to reach Japan, East Asia and India by means of the Western route.

It is beyond question that Columbus was in search of gold, much gold. But it would be a caricature of the real nature of his efforts if we were to claim that Columbus was a materialistic gold-digger. Columbus was following a geo-eschatology current in that time. One hemisphere was the earthly paradise or the garden of Eden: the ideal of primal times and the eschatological goal of the end of times. The history of humankind began there in a state of perfection and that was also the scene of the first human sin. Eden was the precise centre of one hemisphere. The centre, the antipode, of the other hemisphere was Jerusalem, to which Adam was expelled after he had sinned. Columbus saw the finding of Eden or Paradise as an indication that human history was coming to an end. In his view the two geographical areas must be brought together: both must be in the hands of Christians before Christ's return. Because the king of Spain now exercised rule over paradise (the areas occupied by Columbus), it was logical and a prophetic task for the king also to bring the other pole, Jerusalem, under his rule. By ruling both poles or centres, the king would be the last ruler of the world, according to the prophecies. Discovery, evangelization and the development of the riches of the New World had to precede a crusade for the conquest of Jerusalem. The riches – the gold – of the New World were to be used to conquer Jerusalem. Columbus confirmed his vison that the fruits of his voyages were destined to restore the holy temple in Jerusalem in a letter to Pope Alexander VI.[2]

Columbus maintained close links with the Franciscan order in Spain. His affinity with them is shown above all in his missionary pictures. Thus he came into contact with apocalyptic enthusiastic members of the Observant reform within this order. He did not criticize church, state and society, but he did emphasize that the existing church and state should have as powerful a role as possible. An important phase of prophecy was fulfilled by the discovery of new lands and new peoples. The eschatological clock would soon stop ticking. The following phases would begin soon, since the world would only last another 150 years. First the gospel had to be spread through the world, and then Jerusalem had to be conquered and the holy temple rebuilt on Mount Zion by the Spanish king. The last days – and the biblical chronology relating to them – would begin with these events. The new heaven and new earth were not far away. Columbus trusted in the guidance of the Holy Spirit, and he was convinced that he had received a spiritual understanding. This guided him more than any other knowledge of a profane kind.[3]

It was between 13 September 1501 and 23 March 1502 (in the period between the third and fourth voyages) that Columbus wrote his *Book of Prophecies*. The real title is longer and clearer: *A Book about the Authoritative Statements, Words, Opinions and Prophecies concerning the Regaining of the Holy City and Mountain of God, Zion, and the Discovery and Conversion of the Islands of India and of all Peoples and Nations, presented to Ferdinand and Elisabeth, Our Spanish King and Queen*.[4] The Latin text and an English translation with extensive commentaries has recently been published.[5] At first sight the work seems to be a great collection of quotations, as if it were the result of a hobby. Forty-three books of the Bible, twenty-one classical and early Christian writers and thirty-three mediaeval works are quoted by Columbus. This does not mean that he had read them all himself, since he was able to make use of other collections of texts. However, this does not detract from the fact that he was very well read in Christian, Jewish and Islamic sources.

In expounding the Bible Columbus used the theory of a twofold literal meaning: events which took place in the Old Testament were a foreshadowing of events which took place in the New Testament. Thus as well as a physical world map he also had a spiritual world map in his luggage. In his own words, the latter was more important than the former: 'Continually, without a moment's hesitation, the Scriptures urge me to press forward with great haste.'[6] But God also was in a hurry: 'I said above that much of the prophecies remained to be fulfilled, and I believe that these are great events for the world. I believe that there is evidence that our Lord is hastening these things. This evidence is the fact that the Gospel must now be proclaimed to so many lands in such a short time.'[7]

The spiritual map of the world in Columbus's luggage was thus connected with the Bible. A few examples may illustrate this. Columbus made a distinction between biblical and other texts dealing with what had already taken place, with what was happening in the present or what would happen in the near future, and with the future or the last days. What had already happened related to the former greatness and fall of Jerusalem, to the prophecies of the rebuilding of Jerusalem and the temple, and the coming of the Antichrist and the last days. Here he made extensive use of Isa. 41–66 and to a lesser degree of Jeremiah, Baruch, Ezekiel, Daniel, Hosea, Joel, Amos and some other minor prophets with the exception of Zechariah, who received more attention. In the geo-eschatology which Columbus shared with his contemporaries here there is a discussion of the antipode of the hemisphere, namely the ruined Jerusalem, with a forward look towards its restoration. The part of Columbus's book which describes the present and the near future analyses Isaiah 1–33, I and II Chronicles, some quotations from Matthew, Luke and John and commentaries by some church fathers.

The subject is the announcement of salvation to all peoples, which was taking place in Columbus's day and which was a herald of the end. Part Four is about the future or the last days. Here one is struck by the minutious search through a great many books of the Bible to collect texts about foreign islands, which are said to be waiting patiently for their redemption, after which they will bring gifts and sacrifices of gold to the new Jerusalem. It is also striking that all this is related to the islands which Columbus had discovered in this other hemisphere. So Columbus could write that he was convinced that the Lord had something clearly miraculous in view with the discovery of and voyages to the Indies and that the king of Spain had to believe in his call in order to connect it with that other project: the conquest of Jerusalem by a crusade and the rebuilding of the temple.[8] Columbus's spiritual map of the world is very strongly governed by the Bible and above all by the prophet Isaiah.

2. Bartolomé de Las Casas and the messianic programme

Ten years after Columbus, Las Casas landed on Hispaniola. In 1502 he could already see the destructive consequences of the conquest. In 1514 – meanwhile he had been ordained priest – he was convinced that the whole Spanish system of the conquest and exploitation of the Indians was unjust, and he resolved to change the system. Eight years later, in 1522, he entered the Dominican Order on Hispaniola. At that moment he already had the title and the task of Protector of the Indians. Up to his death in 1566 he tried to fulfil this task through writings, journeys to Spain and experiments in Latin America. Las Casas was a great admirer of Columbus and he took care that the Columbus's ship's diary of 1492–93 should be preserved for us.[9]

According to Las Casas, the divine Lord had chosen the great and illustrious Columbus from among the children of Adam to bring about one of the most eminent achievements of his century. Las Casas knew that Columbus was possessed by the thought that God had found him worthy in one way or another to help in the regaining of the Holy Sepulchre and that Columbus asked Queen Isabella to make a promise to grant the kingdoms gathered in the conquest to the land and sacred house of Jerusalem which was again to be conquered.[10] Las Casas had no problems with the fact that in his time the world had meanwhile become so large and so many people had to be evangelized. He, too, had no objection to people being brought under the Spanish crown. But the war, bloodshed and slavery by which all this was in fact being done found a fervent opponent in him. He stood up for the human rights of the Indians, for conversion by conviction, for an alternative system of government and for an approach which was in accord with the demand of the gospel.

For him, 'Bible and conquest' became 'gospel and violence'. What is striking in Las Casas is that he gives a major role to philosophical and theological arguments. One does not come across quotations from the Gospels very often. Las Casas was arguing in quite a different context from Columbus. He was engaged in a great public debate with opponents who came from these circles or were influenced by these circles. Certainly Las Casas constantly refers to the teaching and practice of Jesus. This comes out strongly above all in his work *On the Only Way in Which All Peoples May be Called to the True Religion* (of which only Chapter 5 has survived). The inhabitants of what Las Casas, too, calls India must be converted, but in a way which accords with the words and actions of Jesus. Two quotations from the Gospels are vigorously put forward by Las Casas. From Luke 4.16–20 he comes to the conclusion that Jesus wanted to evangelize the poor, preached freedom to the captives and gave sight to the blind. No single human power may punish idolatry or any sin, certainly not with death: the message of the Gospels is one of life which may never be destroyed, because Jesus came that human beings might have life to the full. Matthew 10.14–15 makes it clear that Jesus did not give his apostles power to punish those who drove them from their cities. Jesus told them to go away and shake the dust of such cities from off their feet. Evangelization calls for goodness, restraint from any form of compulsion, and patience. Las Casas asked himself: why do so many ravenous wolves and cruel tyrants come to India? Fifty years after his arrival in the New World, in his *Short Account of the Devastation of the Lands of West India*, he wrote: 'I swear to God and my conscience – and I say this as my firm conviction, at whatever length I write about it – that I have not cited and described the ten-thousandth part of all devastations, all damage done to the land, all murder, all acts of violence and other abominations and cruelties which are practised in all these lands, and which from day to day are still being practised throughout India.'[11]

According to Las Casas there is no relation whatsoever between the gospel and violence. In him, Columbus's euphoria gives place to a prophetic and messianic indignation. He stood in the midst of real history, which was a history of suffering, and in so doing discovered the authentic proclamation and the liberating actions of Jesus of Nazareth.

3. Bernardino de Sahagún: idolatry is an invention of the devil

At the age of thirty, after a university training and having become a Franciscan, Sahagún came to Mexico, where he was to remain for around sixty years – from 1529 to 1590. In this long period he achieved a unique work. He recorded all the culture of the Aztecs in all its aspects as an accomplished ethnographer, with the help of well-educated Aztec informants. He recorded it all in Aztec and Spanish. His missiological method consisted of three phases: first a thorough study of the language of the people; then a scientific investigation and precise recording of all religious, cultural and secular insights, rites and customs; and finally the translation of prayers, Gospels, etc. and also the writing of catechisms, books of sermons and handbooks for missionaries. He did pioneering work in all these areas. That does not mean that his method of evangelization was universally approved of. Sahagún criticized the method of the first missionaries, and the Spanish authorities were anxious that this thorough information would bring back the earlier view of life and spheres of power. Moreover his greatest work, *General History of the*

Things of New Spain, was to remain forgotten until the end of the last century.[12]

The question is, why did Sahagún reconstruct the old culture so thoroughly and so comprehensively? We cannot exclude the possibility that as a scholar he himself needed to gather knowledge. But he was also a very convinced and steadfast bringer of the good news. That is evident from the prologues and the interpolations that he wrote. In the actual text of the twelve volumes Sahagún remains extremely matter-of-fact and tries to give an objective indication of what he discovered through his informants and his own investigations, and these texts are almost exclusively in two columns, in Nahuatl and Spanish. The prologues and the interpolations are in Spanish. Just once there is an appendix, in Book 1, and then again Nahuatl and Spanish are used. To discover Sahagún's own views one has to make use of the prologues, interpolations and appendices.

In the prologue of his first book, *The Gods*, Sahagún points out that a good doctor must have a knowledge of medicines and illnesses in order to be able to find the right cure for every ailment. That is also the case with preachers and confessors who must cure spiritual ailments. The ailments are the sins of idolatry: idolatrous rituals, idolatrous superstitions, sooth-sayings, abuses and idolatrous ceremonies which have not yet been completely rooted out. To cure these and to know whether they still exist it is necessary to know how they were present in the period of the idolatry, i.e. earlier. Sahagún explicitly states that he has written the twelve books for this reason.[13]

At various places Sahagún goes more deeply into this idolatry. In this respect he is a child of his time. In the theology of those days – and this goes back over a long history – other religions were the work of the devil. Idolatry is related to polytheism. Sometimes heavenly bodies and elements are worshipped as gods, sometimes it is ancestors who are divinized, and sometimes even unclean and dirty animals. So people make idols and worship them. Behind all this stands the devil, who is jealous of the divine omnipotence and burns with desire to be worshipped as God. The devil imitates what God has brought into being in the worship he has willed and thus leads people astray in order to receive divine honour. People who allow themselves to be deceived by the devil are destined for hell. In an interpolation in his second book Sahagún writes that people must not be regarded harshly, because they are the victims of our most cruel enemy Satan, who in the most crafty way leads them astray into such infernal actions. Sahagún ends with an urgent prayer: Lord, take away from him any power to do evil![14]

At the end of the first book Sahagún writes a long and remarkable appendix. It is addressed to the inhabitants of Mexico. Sahagún gives a description of many sorts of idolatry, but he also writes that all this amounts to a misunderstanding of the creation by the one God of all that exists. When the world began there were no idolaters, and before the world passes away, idolatry will have disappeared. In the meantime the devil is at work. He is the cause of idolatry, and God has no mercy on him. He taught human beings to make idols, to worship the sun and holy places, to sacrifice human beings and cultivate all kinds of immorality. In this way the world of the Indians came about. They became enslaved to all this and could only be made to desist from it by the vassals of God, the Christians: the Christians conquered them!

Then follows a long and urgent prayer in which Sahagún prays God to show his power and to conquer the devil. After that Sahagún begins a refutation of the idolatry in the form of an address to the inhabitants of Mexico. The tone is not harsh. He addresses them as 'my children'. He makes only one reference to the word of God in the Bible, and in so doing bases himself on the book of Wisdom. He uses many arguments to show that there is only one God. But this is a God who is concerned for everyone and everything. All the gods of the Aztecs are brought forward and are clearly told: 'You are no god.' All the gods of the peoples are demons, devils or evil spirits. Sahagún is disturbed when he thinks of how many lies, how much deception and betrayal, the devil is inflicting on people and how much suffering they are incurring. Sahagún asks God: 'Why have you not wanted so many people to know you for so long?' He prays God to seize and imprison the devil so that he can never threaten people again in this way.[15]

In Sahagún, Bible and conquest are developed as a struggle between God and the devil. It may seem amazing that so great a scholar with such results which defy the centuries should have been carrying around such theological baggage. His great knowledge and his deep insight into the world of the Aztecs did not help him to doubt this theology. Sahagún was deeply rooted in the theology of his day. But he did not go so far as to make the people of Mexico personally responsible. He exonerated them, and through his record of the whole of their culture, he and his fellow brothers saw to it that a symbiosis, a juxtaposed religion of old and new, could arise. It was the people in Mexico who brought that about: an Aztec-Christian form of religion.

4. Retrospect

'Bible and Conquest' seems to uncover a complicated and ambiguous process in the sixteenth century. The euphoric Columbus created a vision embracing past, present and future on the basis of the prophecies: the conquest was at the service of regaining Jerusalem and of the end of the ages. Las Casas was inspired by the messianic Gospel texts: the cruel mentality of the Spanish conquerors must be undone by discipleship of the earthly Jesus and the liberation of the people of New Spain. Sahagún interprets his experience of the New World in terms of the book of Wisdom as a continuous struggle between God and the devil or as a reconquest from the devil of God's originally good creation. Again scripture seems to be more than text.

Translated by John Bowden

Notes

1. W. Cantwell Smith, *What is Scripture? A Comparative Approach*, London and Minneapolis 1993, 223, 232–8.
2. *The Libro de las Profecías of Christopher Columbus. An en face edition.* Translation and commentary by Delno C. West and August Kling, Gainesville 1991, 68f.
3. Ibid., 27–36, 55–60.
4. Ibid., 100.
5. Cf. n. 2 above.
6. Ibid., 105.
7. Ibid., 111.
8. Ibid., 107, 111.
9. Cristobal Colon, *Diary of Christopher Columbus's First Voyage to America, 1492–93*, Oklahoma 1991.
10. *Witness. Writings of Bartolomé de Las Casas*, edited and translated by George Sanderlin, Maryknoll 1992, 29, 31; G. Gutiérrez, *Las Casas. In Search of the Poor of Jesus Christ*, Maryknoll 1993, passim.
11. Bartolomé de Las Casas, *Short Account of the Destruction of the Indies*, ed. A. R. Pagden, Harmondsworth 1992; Gutiérrez, *Las Casas*, 160ff.; Bartolomé de Las Casas, *The Only Way*, ed. Helen Rand Paris, Mahwah, NJ 1992, 77, 86.
12. Bernardino de Sahagún, *Florentine Codex. General History of the Things of New Spain*, translated from the Aztec by A. J. O. Anderson and C. E. Dibble, Santa Fé 1950–1974 (12 vols); Miguel Leon-Portilla, *Bernardino de Sahagún*, Madrid 1987.
13. *Florentine Codex, Part I: Introductions and Indices. Introductions, Sahagún's Prologues and Interpolations, General Bibliography, General Indices*, ed. A. J. O. Anderson and C. E. Dibble, Santa Fé 1982, 45f.
14. Ibid., 57f.; A. Camps, 'Begegnung mit indianischen Religionen; Wahrnehmung und Beurteilung in der Kolonialzeit', in *Conquista und Evangelisation. Fünfhundert Jahre Orden in Lateinamerika*, ed. M. Sievernich, A. Camps, A. Müller and W. Seener, Mainz 1992, 348–72; M. Delgado, 'Von der Verteufelung zur Anerkennung durch Umdeutung. Der "Wandel" in der Beurteilung der indianischen

Religionen durch die christliche Theologie im 16. und 17. Jahrhundert', *Neue Zeitschrift für Missionswissenschaft* 49, 1993, 257–89.

15. Bernardino de Sahagún, *Florentine Codex. General History of the Things of New Spain, 1. The Gods* (cf. n. 12 above), 1970, 53–76.

III · From Scroll to Book of Life: The Bible as Source of Human Values

New Ways of Reading the Bible in the Cultural Settings of the Third World

Jean-Pierre Ruiz

When the day of Pentecost had come, they were all together in one place . . . All of them were filled with the Holy Spirit and began to speak in other languages, as the Spirit gave them ability . . . And at this sound the crowd gathered and was bewildered, because each one heard them speaking in the native language of each. Amazed and astonished, they asked, 'Are not all these who are speaking Galileans? And how is it that we hear, each of us, in our own native language? Parthians, Medes, Elamites, and residents of Mesopotamia, Judea and Cappadocia, Pontus and Asia, Phrygia and Pamphylia, Egypt and the parts of Libya belonging to Cyrene, and visitors from Rome, both Jews and proselytes, Cretans and Arabs – in our own languages we hear them speaking about God's deeds of power.' All were amazed and perplexed, saying to one another, 'What does this mean?'

These words from Acts 2.1–13 provide a fitting overture to this reflection on new ways of reading the Bible that are developing in the diverse cultural contexts of the Third World. For the Parthians, Medes, Elamites, and all who understood the gospel that Pentecost day, today we might substitute Thais, Malawians, African-Americans, Pakistanis, Brazilians, South Africans, Argentinians and so many others who are hearing the Bible in their own languages and claiming their own voices to speak about God's deeds of power. Like those who heard the apostolic proclamation at Pentecost, we now ask, 'What does this mean?'

Prior considerations of this question include *Unexpected News: Reading the Bible with Third World Eyes*, a 1984 study by Robert McAfee Brown, a pre-eminent interpreter of Third World (especially Latin American) theologies for United States audiences.[1] Likewise, in *Liberat-*

ing Exegesis: The Challenge of Liberation Theology to Biblical Studies, written in Great Britain, Christopher Rowland and Mark Corner outlined what Third World biblical interpretations (especially Latin America and South Africa) might contribute to liberation theology in the First World.[2]

Much has happened in Third World biblical interpretation in the decade since Brown's book. Developments over the course of the decade have made the designation of such readings as 'Third World' even more problematic than it was in 1984. Theologically, it might be said that the parents of Third World biblical interpretation, mostly Latin American, are now grandparents of broadening global circles of exegetical and theological discourse. Clear signals of this are provided in *Voices from the Margin: Interpreting the Bible in the Third World*, edited by R. S. Sugirtharajah.[3] The thirty-three essays in that anthology are organized into five parts which accurately reflect the *status quaestionis* of biblical interpretation among Third World readers: 1. use of the Bible: principles, and issues; 2. re-use of the Bible: examples of hermeneutical explorations; 3. the Exodus: one theme, many perspectives; 4. one reality, many texts: examples of multi-faith hermeneutics; 5. people as exegetes. The authors are Africans, African-Americans, Asians, Latin Americans and Native Americans – a spectrum that reflects the variety of contexts and the diversity of readings now laying claim to serious consideration in the Church and in the academy.

In the following pages, I will present a sampling of ways in which Third World interpreters are presenting new readings of the Bible. I will also address some of the ways in which Third World biblical interpretation has begun to make a difference in the church and in the academy in the First World.

1. Third World readings: models, methods and challenges

In *Mañana: Christian Theology from a Hispanic Perspective*, Justo L. González, a Cuban American Methodist theologian, coined 'reading the Bible in Spanish' as a metaphor for biblical interpretation in the Hispanic context as a vernacular reading 'not only in the cultural, linguistic sense but also in the sociopolitical sense. In the high Andes, the equivalent of our reading in Spanish would be a reading in Quechua, and from the perspective of the Quechua-speaking peoples oppressed by the Spanish-speaking.'[4] Powerful and challenging readings are emerging thoughout the Third World as interpreters work to construct 'grammars' for such readings in their own vernaculars.

Voices from the Margin provides two examples of Korean readings of the Bible, Cyrus H. Moon's 'A Korean Minjung Perspective: The Hebrews and the Exodus', reprinted from his book, *A Korean Minjung Theology: An Old Testament Perspective* (1985);[5] and Ahn Byung-Mu's 'Jesus and the Minjung in the Gospel of Mark', from a volume edited by the Commission on Theological Concerns of the Christian Conference of Asia entitled *Minjung Theology: People as the Subjects of History* (1981).[6] As Kwok Pui Lan explains, '*Minjung* is a Korean word which means the mass of people, or the mass who were subjugated or being ruled . . . They were treated as either docile or as mere spectators of the rise and fall of kingdoms. *Minjung* theology, however, reclaims *minjung* as protagonists in the historical drama.'[7]

Reading the Exodus side by side with the events of Korean history according to a *minjung* 'grammar' leads Cyrus H. S. Moon to construct a dialogical reading. This yields the insight that 'In Exodus 3 God is revealed as a liberator first, as one who would liberate God's *minjung* from bondage and settle them in a land of their own.'[8] Moon's reading makes the Exodus accessible in the Korean context: he sees that the *habiru* were among the *minjung* of their time. It is their *han*, that is, their resentment born of innocent suffering, that propelled them into action against the injustices to which they were subjected.[9] Without denying the cultural and historical distance between the Exodus and Korean history, Moon recognizes that Korean Christians 'found the God of the Exodus most meaningful for their historical situation'.[10]

Ahn Byung-Mu's Korean contextual reading makes him sensitive to an otherwise usually neglected feature of Mark's Gospel, namely, the crowds who are Jesus' main audience. He employs the tools of Western historical-critical exegesis in the service of a Korean contextual reading of Mark.[11] Sensitivity to the *minjung* leads him to attend to Mark's distinctive use of *ochlos* and to identify these crowds as a downtrodden group contrasted with the ruling class. Though they are the outcasts of society – not a class, but a polymorphous group including sinners, tax collectors and the sick – those who belong to the *ochlos* are privileged recipients of Jesus' unconditional acceptance.

Beyond reshaping Western methods for their own readings, Third World interpreters are also bringing methods to bear on biblical study which were developed in the context of indigenous, non-Christian religious traditions. In 'Water – God's Extravaganza: John 2.1–11', Sister Vandana, an Indian biblical scholar, uses the *Dhvani* method of exegesis drawn from the study of Sanskrit religious texts to interpret the sign at the wedding feast of Cana. Sugirtharajah's introduction to that essay explains the aesthetic and affective emphases of *Dhvani* interpretation.[12] Thus, for example, Sister Vandana understands the figure of Mary in John 2.1–11 in terms drawn from Indian tradition: 'Mary is someone who taught by her *maun vyakhya* (silent discourse).'[13] Exploring the symbolism of water in John 2, Sister Vandana finds some of the prayers addressed to the waters of the Ganges river reminiscent of prayers Christians address to Mary: 'Who can describe, O Mother, thy glory and splendour? O, all powerful mother of compassion and love!'[14]

Important signs of the diversification in Third World biblical interpretation are found in essays by Naim Stifan Ateek and Robert Allen Warrior, both of which challenge the paradigmatic prominence of the Exodus story in Third World theologies. In *A Theology of Liberation*, Gustavo Gutiérrez wrote, 'The Exodus experience is paradigmatic. It remains vital and contemporary due to similar historical experiences which the People of God undergo.'[15] In *Exodus: A Hermeneutics of Freedom*, J. Severino Croatto described the Exodus event as 'a characteristic, provocative, creative, inexhaustible kerygmatic "locus"'.[16] However, in 'A Palestinian Perspective: The Bible and Liberation', Naim Stifan Ateek points to ways in which the biblical story of the Exodus and the biblical promise of the land have been used as tools of oppression rather than as resources for liberation. According to Ateek, 'Liberation theologians have seen the Bible as a dynamic source for their understanding of liberation, but if some parts of it are applied literally to our situation today the Bible appears to offer the Palestinians slavery rather than freedom.'[17] Reading the Exodus and Conquest narratives from the standpoint of the Canaanites yields a far different picture from readings focused on the Israelites alone.

Another challenge to the Exodus paradigm is framed by Robert Allen Warrior in 'A Native American Perspective: Canaanites, Cowboys and Indians'. As a member of the Osage Nation of American Indians, Warrior reads the Exodus in sympathy with the Canaanites indigenous to the land in which the Israelites were newcomers. While he recognizes the complex inter-relationships between the Conquest narrative and the events of history, it is the Conquest narrative that Warrior finds disturbing, for he reads there the story of how God the deliverer became God the conqueror. Tragically, Warrior notes, many people who reclaim the Exodus narratives as paradigmatic stories of liberation 'ignore those parts of the story that describe Yahweh's command mercilessly to annihilate the indigenous population'.[18]

Perhaps the most prominent sign of the steadily increasing vitality of Third World biblical interpretation is the emergence of Third World women's readings. While the first generation of Third World theologians were mostly Latin American males, a steadily increasing number of women are now claiming their voices as interpreters of the Bible.[19] In their introduction to *The Will to Arise: Women, Tradition and the Church in Africa*, Mercy Amba Oduyoye and Musimbe R. A. Kanyoro explain that 'African women reading the Bible have begun to see that God's call to them is not passive. It is compelling and compulsory.'[20]

In *With Passion and Compassion: Third World Women Doing Theology* (Maryknoll 1988), a volume of reflections from the Women's Commission of the Ecumenical Association of Third World Theologians (EATWOT) edited by Virginia Fabella and Mercy Amba Oduyoye, the Nigerian New Testament scholar Teresa Okure's essay 'Women in the Bible' reflects on the constitutive significance of Eve.[21] In another essay in the same volume, 'Women's Rereading of the Bible', Elsa Tamez, author of *La Biblia de los oprimidos: La opresión en la teología bíblica* (San José, Costa Rica 1979; English translation Maryknoll, 1982) and editor of *El Rostro Femenino de la Teología* (Costa Rica 1986; English translation Maryknoll 1989) reminds us from a Latin American perspective that the marginalization of women makes for serious 'differences between reading the Bible from the point of view of the poor and reading it from a woman's perspective'.[22] Asian women working to interpret the Bible include the Chinese biblical scholar Kwok Pui Lan and the Korean biblical scholar Lee Oo Chung, whose 'Peace, Unification and Women I. A Bible Study' appears in *We Dare to Dream: Doing Theology as Asian Women*.[23]

2. Third World biblical interpretation and the First World church

In 1992, the fifth centenary of Christopher Columbus' arrival in the Americas provided the backdrop for the Fourth General Conference of the Latin American Bishops (CELAM) in Santo Domingo. The intense controversy surrounding the fifth centenary itself underlined the fact that the evangelization of the Americas forms part of a non-innocent history, a history of colonizers who came carrying both the gospel and the sword, and who all too often used the gospel as a weapon of colonial power far subtler and far sharper than their swords. As the Permanent Council of the Canadian Conference of Catholic Bishops said in their 1992 pastoral message, 'Toward a New Evangelization', 'The story of Christianity in the Americas is not a *levenda negra*, a black legend, but neither is it an impeccable tale of glory.'[24]

In line with the theme 'New Evangelization, Human Development, Christian Culture', following upon the theme of the 1979 Third General

Conference at Puebla, 'Evangelization in Latin America's Present and Future', the Latin American bishops concluded that

> One goal of inculturated evangelization will always be the salvation and integral liberation of a particular people or human group, strengthening its identity and trusting in its specific future. At the same time, it will stand opposed to the power of death by taking on the perspective of Jesus Christ incarnate, who out of weakness, poverty, and the redeeming cross, saved humankind (*Santo Domingo Conclusions*, 243).

In the Americas, the 'new evangelization' can be understood in part as a deliberate response to the growth of biblical fundamentalism, a development noted in alarmist terms by those who wonder aloud whether Latin America is turning Protestant, and in somewhat more measured tones by those who note the increasing outflow of Third World Catholics to fundamentalist groups. In this context, the interpretation of the Bible in Third World churches has begun to attract urgent attention.

Issued one hundred years after *Providentissimus Deus*, and fifty years after *Divino Afflante Spiritu*, the November 1993 document of the Pontifical Biblical Commission, 'The Interpretation of the Bible in the Church', gives clear evidence that Third World biblical interpretations have begun to make their distinctive mark.[25] The document's survey and evaluation of methods and approaches for biblical interpretation includes a consideration of contextual (liberationist and feminist) approaches, a treatment which the commission prefaces by recognizing that 'the interpretation of a text is always dependent on the mindset and concerns of its readers'. After sketching principles which guide the liberationist approach, the Commission's evaluation begins on a strongly positive note:

> Liberation theology includes elements of undoubted value: the deep awareness of the God who saves; the insistence on the communal dimension of faith; the pressing sense of need for a liberating praxis rooted in justice and love; a fresh reading of the Bible which seeks to make the word of God the light and the nourishment of the people of God in the midst of its struggles and hopes. In all these ways it underlines the capacity of the inspired text to speak to the world of today.

While this appreciation of the fresh readings of the Bible taking place in Third World contexts is tempered by the document's attention to the risks which such new readings can entail, the document's overall evaluation is deliberately tentative: 'Since liberation theology is tied to a movement that is still in a process of development, the remarks which follow can only be provisional.'[26]

The fourth section of the Commission's document, addressing the interpretation of the Bible in the life of the Church, focuses on actualization, inculturation and on the use of the Bible (in the liturgy, in *lectio divina*, in pastoral ministry and in ecumenism). The impact of Third World biblical interpretations emerges here under the heading of inculturation and in the document's reflections on the use of the Bible in pastoral ministry. The Biblical Commission takes a post-colonialist turn, insisting that the process of inculturation

> must be taken up again and again, in relationship to the way in which cultures continue to evolve. In countries of more recent evangelization, the problem arises in somewhat different terms. Missionaries, in fact, cannot help bring the word of God in the form in which it has been inculturated in their own country of origin. New local churches have to make every effort to convert this foreign form of biblical inculturation into another form more closely corresponding to the culture of their own land.

The Biblical Commission's remarks on the use of the Bible in pastoral ministry includes a paragraph which treats the place of the Bible in *comunidades eclesiales de base*, basic Christian communities. In this context, the Commission recognizes that

> there is reason to rejoice in seeing the Bible in the hands of people of lowly condition and of the poor; they can bring to its interpretation and to its actualization a light more penetrating, from the spiritual and existential point of view, than that which comes from a learning that relies upon its own resources alone (cf. Matt. 11.25).

Here, at one and the same time, the Biblical Commission affirms the epistemological privilege of the poor and the marginalized (a consistent emphasis of Third World biblical hermeneutics) and subverts the hermeneutical hegemony of First World academic elites. In that respect, it furnishes a partial response to concerns raised in the introduction to the document, where the Commission notes that biblical interpretation now 'requires such technical refinements as to render it a domain reserved for a few specialists alone'. As a result, some level the charge of Luke 11.52 against the academic exegetical elite: 'Woe to you lawyers! You have taken away the key of knowledge; you did not enter yourselves, and you hindered those who were entering.'

3. Third World biblical interpretation and the First World academy

The success of Third World biblical interpretation is not to be judged according to the conformity of its practitioners to First World standards. There is growing evidence that Third World biblical interpretations have begun to pry open the door to exert their own influence on academic discourse in First World settings. For example, EATWOT includes members who belong to racial and ethnic minorities in the United States: African-Americans, Asian Americans, Hispanic-Americans and Native-Americans. This participation recognizes that the histories and experiences of racial and ethnic minorities in the US give them common cause with marginalized peoples around the globe. Just as importantly, it also advances the cross-contextual conversations among them.

With specific regard to the impact of Third World biblical interpretation on the academic study of the Bible in the First World, another positive indicator is the formation of the 'Bible in Africa, Asia and Latin America Group' as a programme unit at the annual meetings of the Society of Biblical Literature. During the 1992 SBL meeting in San Francisco, California, the group focused on the theme 'Reading the Bible in This Place: Texts in Asian Contexts'. The presentations included Khiok-Khng Yeo on 'The Rhetorical Hermeneutic of I Corinthians 8 for Chinese Ancestor Worship', Barbara Bowe's 'Reading Paul Through Filipino Eyes', and Hisako Kinukawa's 'A Feminist Interpretation of Mark 5.25–34 in the Japanese Context'. The group's second session was devoted to a panel review of *Voices from the Margin*. At another session, Elsa Tamez presented 'Quetzalcóatl Challenges the Christians' Bible'. Her paper spotlighted the challenge posed to biblical hermeneutics by the emergent efforts of native Latin American peoples to recover their ancestral spiritual legacies.

At the 1993 meeting of the SBL in Washington, DC, the group focused its attention on 'Popular and Academic Interpretation of the Bible: What Meeting Place and Whose Terms?'. Offering African, Asian and Central American perspectives, the presentations included 'Reading the Bible in African Contexts: Works in Progress', by Justin Ukpong and John K. Riches; 'Reading the Image of Jesus into the Old Testament in the Korean Church', by Sok-chung Chang; and 'An Academic Appraisal of Popular Uses of Eschatological Terms in Korean Christian Communities' by Joon Ho (Amos) Chang. Panelists M. Daniel Carroll R. of the Seminario Teológico Centroamericano in Guatemala and Irene Foulkes of the Seminario Bíblico Latinoamericano in Costa Rica discussed the session's theme from a Central American perspective. For 1994, the group's focus is 'Text and Texts in a Multifaith Context', inviting attention to ways of relating the Bible to the sacred texts and traditions of non-Christian religions.

The presence of Third World voices in the First World academy, exemplified by this SBL group, establishes a pluralism that will not be tamed and that refuses to remain peripheral. Confronting the hermeneutical challenge of a pluralistic, polycentric world, David Tracy insists that readings by the oppressed are those that 'the rest of us need most to hear', so as to build a foundation for active solidarity with those who articulate such readings.[27] Furthermore, Third World interpreters of the Bible demonstrate qualities of commitment and engagement that challenge First World interpreters to critical reflection on the ways in which their own commitments are mirrored in their interpretative practices. Articles by David Jobling and Daniel Patte are promising indicators that this has begun to take place.

In 'Writing the Wrongs of the World: The Deconstruction of the Biblical Text in the Context of Liberation Theologies', Jobling examines the critical relationship between liberation and deconstruction, concluding that 'both liberation and deconstruction challenge biblical specialists to develop . . . multiple vision and commitment'.[28] In 'Textual Constraints, Ordinary Readings and Critical Exegeses: An Androcritical Perspective', Patte rethinks the often antagonistic relationship between ordinary readings of biblical texts and readings by the academic exegetical elite.[29] That rethinking reflects Patte's attention to Third World interpreters' insistence on the hermeneutical privilege of the poor, the marginalized, the oppressed.

Both Jobling and Patte include deliberately self-conscious and self-critical reflection as an indispensable element in the interpretative equation. This sort of attention to the interpreter is a factor which Third World theologians and feminist theologians have highlighted as a key to understanding the underpinnings of all understanding and interpretation as contextual. Attention to the interpreter's social location has meant stripping away the veneer of detached, disinterested objectivism from academic discourse in an honest effort to lay bare the complex web of presuppositions, commitments and constituencies that shape the process of reading. Stepping out into vulnerability from behind the screen of neutrality renders interpreters more explicitly accountable for their readings, in the churches and in the academy.

4. Continuing conversations, continuing challenges

When the crowds at Pentecost realized that they heard and understood, they began to converse with each other in their own language. That second miracle may be just as astonishing as the first. In his 'Postscript: Achievements and Items for a Future Agenda', R. S. Sugirtharajah concludes *Voices from the Margin* by insisting, 'The time has come for Asian, Latin American and black hermeneuts to start conversing among themselves. This is probably one of the most urgent tasks before them.'[30] Until recently, the preoccupation of Third World biblical interpreters has been to create space for their own distinctive discourses, apart from the preoccupations of the First World. For Sugirtharajah, at least two challenges specify the urgency of dialogue among Third World interpreters: 1. the need to clarify such undeclared tensions as the status and authority of the Bible in the interpreters' respective contexts; 2. the need to overcome the interpreters' tendency to absolutize the concerns that emerge from their own contexts.

The diversity of the discourses in which Third World biblical interpreters are engaging is becoming more evident as the conversation among them becomes more self-conscious and more deliberately self-critical. As that conversation continues, its very diversity is likely to address Sugirtharajah's second concern, even if only indirectly. Hearing the Bible read in another's vernacular, and conversing with the other, provides some measure of prevention against the illusion that one's own vernacular is the universal and normative context for legitimate biblical interpretation.

The tensions between academic and popular readings of the Bible pose yet another challenge to Third World biblical interpretation. Professional biblical scholars with one foot in the academy and the other foot in the community must advance the dialogue between these audiences, for each needs to hear the challenges of the other. Taking a step beyond the mixture of enchantment and surprise with which the insights of Carlos Mesters' 'The Use of the Bible in Christian Communities of the Common People' were received, professional biblical scholars need to recognize the stimulus which such readings represent, for the technical tools and the jargon-laden prose which mark the academic vernacular guarantee neither the accuracy nor the value of academic biblical exegesis.[31]

Reminded by Mesters that 'the principal objective of reading the Bible is not to interpret the Bible but to interpret life with the help of the Bible',[32] academic interpreters are in a position to invite attention to the tension between the immediacy and the otherness of the biblical text. That tension serves as a corrective against facile over-identification between interpreter and text, against the one-dimensional readings symptomatic of fundamentalist interpretation. It also protects against the domestication of the biblical text, preserving its power to transform, to serve as a vehicle of God's restless and transformative Spirit.

Notes

1. Philadelphia 1984.
2. London and Louisville 1989.
3. London and Maryknoll 1991.
4. Nashville 1990, 84–5. See J. P. Ruiz, 'Beginning to Read the Bible in Spanish: An Initial Assessment', *Journal of Hispanic/Latino Theology* 1. 2, February 1994, 28–50.
5. *Voices from the Margin*, 241–55.
6. Ibid., 85–103.
7. 'Discovering the Bible in the Non-Biblical World', in *Voices from the Margin*, 307.
8. 'A Korean Minjung Perspective: The Hebrews and the Exodus', 244.
9. Ibid., 242. Moon directs his readers to S. Nam Dong, 'Towards a Theology of *Han*', in *Minjung Theology: People as the Subjects of History*, ed. Commission on Theological Concerns of the Christian Conference of Asia, Maryknoll and London 1983, 55ff.
10. 'A Korean Minjung Perspective', 253.
11. 'Jesus and the Minjung in the Gospel of Mark', in *Voices from the Margin*, 241–55.
13. Ibid., 121.
14. Ibid., 120–1.
15. Maryknoll 1973, 159 (*Teología de la Liberación*, Lima 1971).
16. Maryknoll 1981, 12 (*Liberación y libertad: pautas hermenéuticas*, Lima 1978).
17. *Voices from the Margin*, 280–6.
18. 'A Native American Perspective', 289–90.
19. See C. F. Parvey, 'Third World Women and Men: Effects of Cultural Change on Interpretation of Scripture', in *The Church and Women in the Third World*, ed. J. C. B. and E. L. Webster, Philadelphia 1985, 105–19.
20. Maryknoll 1992, 1.
21. *With Passion and Compassion*, 47–59.
22. Ibid., 174.
23. Maryknoll 1990, 65–71. First published by the Asian Women's Resource Centre for Culture and Theology and the Asian Office of the Women's Commission of EATWOT (Hong Kong 1989).
24. *Origins* 22, 1992, 286.
25. English text in *The Interpretation of the Bible in the Church*, ed. J. L. Houlden, London 1995.
26. The Biblical Commission cautions liberationist interpreters against the construction of a narrowly focused canon within the canon, against dependence on materialist analytical tools and models, and against the over-emphasis on earthly eschatology that can emerge as a logical consequence of overwhelming social problems.
27. *Plurality and Ambiguity: Hermeneutics, Religion, Hope*, San Francisco and London 1987, 104, 105–107.

28. *Semeia* 51, 1990, 109.

29. *Semeia* 62, 1993, 59–79.

30. *Voices from the Margin*, 443.

31. In *The Challenge of Basic Christian Communities*, ed. S. Torres and J. Eagleson, Maryknoll 1981, 197–210.

32. As cited in Rowland and Corner, *Liberating Exegesis*, 39.

The Bible as Magna Carta of Movements for Liberation and Human Rights

George M. Soares-Prabhu

One of the striking contributions of the Bible to the contemporary world has been the profusion of liberation theologies it has inspired. In the last fifty years, biblically-based theologies of liberation have irrupted everywhere in Third World Christianity, and in the oppressed sectors of the Christian First World. The role of the Bible in these theologies of liberation is well known, and does not need to be taken up again. What has been less noticed, and may be worth exploring, is the part the Bible has played in the movement for human rights, which runs parallel to these liberation theologies and, like them, has done much to illumine the dark side of history.

But human rights, unlike liberation, are not a biblical category. For, like most pre-modern religious texts, the Bible speaks the language of duties rather than of rights. And the human rights movement too, unlike liberation theology, is not a Christian movement. It has developed outside the church and to a large extent in opposition to it.[1] Yet the rights spelled out in the UN Declaration of Human Rights, and accepted (in principle at least) everywhere, are rooted in values that the Bible has contributed to Western society. In this sense human rights are in part a legacy of the Bible. But they are a legacy of the Bible as a cultural document rather than as a religious book. It is this legacy that I try to assess here by 1. examining how human rights are understood today and 2. asking what the Bible has to say about them.

1. What is wrong with human rights?

Controversy has accompanied the human rights movement from the start, because the notion of 'human rights' is a product of the modern, secular West, and carries with it the biases of its origins.[2] Its remote roots may reach back to the Stoic 'natural law', according to which each thing had its own inherent value; to the Roman *ius gentium* ('law of nations') which, beyond the rights of Roman citizenship, recognized rights accorded by nature to every human being (unless enslaved); and, above all, to the biblical affirmation of the value of the human person as created in the 'image of God'.[3] Its more immediate origins can be traced to 'the notions of "civil rights" and "civil liberties" which began to be developed in the domestic law of England in the seventeenth century, and found their first full flowering, almost simultaneously, in the French *Déclaration des droits de l'homme et du citoyen* and the US Bill of Rights of 1791'.[4] But the concept of international human rights as we have them today appeared only after, and as a result of, the Second World War. Because of the horrors perpetrated by the Nazi state on its own citizens, international law was forced to break out of its self-imposed limits. It began to legislate not just about inter-state relationships between sovereigns (whether sovereign princes or sovereign nation states), but even about the proper relationships that must obtain within a state between the people and their government. The result was that 'a completely new legal code, enumerating and closely defining certain very specific "human rights" and "fundamental freedoms" for all human beings anywhere in the world',[5] began to emerge.

Individual freedom versus social need

Understandably this 'new legal code', now embodied in the UN documents on human rights,[6] has been considerably influenced by the Western historical context in which it developed. But it does try to integrate concerns of the socialist and Third Worlds. Recognizing that 'a full delineation of human rights must include both negative immunities from coercion and also positive entitlements to participation in the public spheres of the economy, the state and the world of culture',[7] the Universal Declaration of Human Rights brings together both civil and political rights (articles 2–21) as well as economic, social and cultural rights (articles 22–27). But in doing this, it brings together two sets of rights which are in some sort of opposition to one another, without showing us how this opposition is to be overcome. For civil and political rights are negative rights ('freedom from'), which call for a sharp limitation of intervention by the state; economic, social and cultural rights are positive rights ('the right to'), which often require state intervention for their implementation.[8]

The First World, because of its historical experience of a long struggle for political freedom against the despotism of church and state, understandably makes much of civil and political rights. But it is suspicious of economic, social and cultural rights, which may call for increased state control – even suggesting that these might not be true 'rights' at all, but at most social ideals: goals for altruism, but not enforceable claims of entitlement.[9] Third World societies, on the other hand, which have lived through the very different kind of economic exploitation and cultural alienation imposed on them by these very champions of civil and political rights, have other priorities. They see the satisfaction of basic material needs (economic, social and political rights) as more urgent than the safeguarding of individual freedoms (civil and political rights) – which last, they know, have been (and are being) manipulated against them by colonial and neocolonial powers as 'legitimating instruments in service to unjust domestic, transnational and international orders'.[10] In their First World *avatar* human rights have often become negative defences of privilege instead of being (as the Third World would like them to be) positive instruments of emancipation.

Egocentric versus sociocentric understandings of the human person

These differences are accentuated by the different perceptions of the human person that underlie First and Third World understandings of human rights. First World perceptions of the person-in-society, Richard Schweder has suggested, are typically egocentric and contractual; Third World perceptions are generally sociocentric and organic.[11] That is, persons in the First World normally experience themselves as autonomous individuals, living in a society which is extrinsic to them. Society exists only because of external contractual obligations undertaken by autonomous individuals for their mutual benefit, and does not in any way affect their essential being. It exists only to foster the fulfilment of the individual, regarded as 'a quasi sacred absolute . . . (whose) rights are limited only by the identical rights of other individuals'.[12] Third World cultures, on the other hand, experience people not as autonomous units, interacting freely in society, but as parts of an organic social whole, which is frequently symbolized by the metaphor of the human body.[13] Individuals are related to society as the members of a body are related to one another and to the body as a whole. They are therefore not autonomous but interdependent. People in the Third World, to the extent that they have not succumbed to modernity, tend to be sociocentric personalities, that is, they are individuals who perceive themselves and structure their behaviour in terms of the perceptions and expectations that society has of them.

Because of this, the Universal Declaration of Human Rights is pulled in different directions by First and Third World interpretations, neither of which is able to maintain the fine balance between the individual and societal rights that it envisages. Both sets of rights are, however, rooted in the Bible. Because it is aware of the special dignity invested in every human being, not merely as an individual but as part of humankind, the Bible is able to harmonize, as neither First nor Third World societies have been able to do, respect for the individual with societal concern. We turn, then, to the Bible, to see how this is done.

2. What does the Bible contribute to human rights?

If one reads the Bible without proof-texting, it does not come across as a consistent defender of universal human rights as we understand them today. There are indeed striking 'human rights' passages in the Bible, like the two creation stories with which the Bible begins (Gen. 1.1–2.4a; 2.4b–25), or Paul's affirmation of the radical equality of humankind recreated in Christ (Jew or Greek, slave or free, male or female), which appears near the Bible's end (Gal. 3.28). Such texts affirm in the clearest possible way the inherent dignity and the radical equality of every human being, which is the ultimate basis of all human rights. They have surely played a decisive role in the genesis of human rights, for the dignity and the inherent equality of every human person that they affirm are not self-evident principles. They are certainly not recognized in intrinsically hierarchical societies, like the caste society of India, or the familial societies of Confucian states. The idea of human rights is more indebted to the Judaeo-Christian biblical tradition than is often realized.

Yet when this is said, it must be admitted that the Bible's affirmation of the dignity of the human person is not consistent. It affirms human dignity in the abstract, in primal and in eschatological time. But when it speaks about concrete human existence in history, the Bible not only acknowledges (as it must) the presence of inequality and oppression in a human history coloured by sin, but seems to condone and even encourage it.

The most significant example of this is, of course, the Conquest, the dark side of the Bible's central liberative event, the Exodus. Theologies of liberation seldom reflect on this embarrassing fact, but the truth is that there is no Exodus in the Bible without the Conquest. Israel is liberated from bonded labour in Egypt, and made YHWH's people at Sinai, in order to possess 'the land' (Ex. 6.8). This seizure of the land, we are told, may not have been a military conquest. It could have taken place through the peaceful settling down of pastoral nomads coming in from outside; or through the justified revolt of local Canaanite peasants, oppressed by the aristocracy of the city-states which controlled and taxed them; or through a combination of any of these.[14] But all such conjectural reconstructions are ultimately irrelevant, for what matters is not what actually happened, but how the Bible presents it. It is the biblical *story*, its confessional not its critical history, which gives us the teaching of the Bible; and in this story the settlement in Canaan is presented unambiguously as a devastating conquest.

For according to the biblical story, what gives Israel the land is the forcible dispossession of the indigenous peoples of Canaan of their lands and their lives. Not only must the people of Israel, at YHWH's express command and with YHWH's active help, 'take possession' of the land of the various native peoples of Transjordania and Canaan, whom YHWH has handed over to them (Num. 33.53; Deut. 1.8.21; 4.38; Josh. 1.11; Judg. 2.6); they must 'drive out all the inhabitants of the land' (Num. 33.55), and indeed 'utterly destroy them . . . make no covenant with them . . . show them no mercy' (Deut. 7.2).[15]

Where, then, are the 'human rights' of 'the Hittites, the Girgashites, the Amorites, the Canaanites, the Perizzites, the Hivites, and the Jebusites' (Deut. 7.1) – with whom Third World peoples will instinctively identify because of their own colonial history? Have they no claim to life and property? The answer of the Bible is, of course, that before YHWH they have none. YHWH the creator disposes absolutely of the lives and possessions of all peoples. YHWH will set aside Mount Seir for Esau (Deut. 2.5), the land of the Ammonites for the descendants of Lot (Deut. 2.19), Transjordania and Canaan for Israel – and India of course for the British! Before YHWH, people have no rights at all.

The Bible therefore does not know of 'human rights' as we understand them today. Like most religious codes it is concerned not with rights but with duties. 'No explicit concept of [human rights] is to be found in Jewish law,' writes Paul Sieghart, quoting Haim Cohn, a justice of the supreme court of Israel, for 'the particular structures of Jewish law *qua* religious laws . . . postulates a system of duties rather than a system of rights'.[16] Such sets of duties (like the Ten Commandments), which imply taking care of others and respecting their persons and possessions, function in fact like a bill of rights. To prohibit killing is to affirm the right to life; to prohibit theft affirms the right to one's possessions; to prohibit false witness is to affirm the neighbours right to his good name. Implicitly, then, the Bible (like other religious texts) does safeguard rights – though only within Israel. For the Gentiles, other than the resident aliens who have become a part of the people, are rarely if ever the object of Israel's concern.[17] But the notion of rights, much less of universal rights, does not appear formally anywhere in the Bible.

What, then, is the contribution of the Bible to human rights? It lies, I believe, in two complementary values that the Bible affirms. The Bible 1. announces in its First Testament, and forcefully affirms in its Second, the sacredness of every human person. And 2. it demands, from beginning to end, as one of its most characteristic features, a responsibility for the welfare of the powerless and the needy, with a persistence and a passion that is paralleled in no other religious literature in the world. These teachings of the Bible ground both the individual and societal rights that figure today in the Universal Declaration of Human Rights, whose formulation and acceptance by the United Nations was, I believe, one of the great moments of hope in our human history.

(a) The sacredness of the human person: the foundation of civil and political rights

The sacredness of the human person is, as we have seen, forcefully affirmed in the two creation stories (the Priestly story of Gen. 1.1–24a and the Yahwist story of Gen. 2.4b–25) with which the Bible begins. In both, humankind is obviously the focus of God's creative work. Humankind is clearly set off from the rest of creation as its crowning summit in Gen. 1.26–30, and as the centre round and for which the rest of the world is made in Gen. 2.7–9. This special place of humankind is explicitly defined in the first creation story by its striking pronouncement that humankind has been made in image of God:

So God created humankind (ha'adam) in God's own image;
in the image of God, God created them;
male and female God created them (Gen. 1.27).

What this marvellous incantation affirms is not so much the unique form as the unique role of humankind. Humankind is created to be the steward of God, God's plenipotentiary representative over creation. 'Just as powerful earthly kings, to indicate their claim to dominion, erect an image of themselves in the provinces of their empire where they do not personally appear, so man is placed upon the earth in God's image as God's sovereign emblem.'[18] The biblical text, moreover, makes it clear that this role of stewardship is not assigned to any one individual but to all humankind, for the Hebrew 'adam is here a collective noun. And it is assigned explicitly to humankind as sexually differentiated, forbidding any discrimination between men and women, for the idea of humankind 'finds its full meaning not in the male alone but in man and woman': male and female God created them.[19]

All this contrasts strikingly with the *Purusha-Sukta*, the celebrated hymn of Rig Veda (X.90), which describes the creation of the cosmos through the dismemberment of the primal human person (*purusha*), who is made the victim in the primal sacrifice. In this extraordinary text, which has become the basis of Hinduism's hierarchical understanding of humankind, we are told that:

His mouth became the priest (*brahman*);
his arms the warrior-prince (*kshatriya*);
his thighs the common people (*vaishya*);
and from his feet the serf (*shudra*) was born (X.90.12).

Suggestions have been made that all that this text is really affirming is the unity and equality of humankind, since all ranks are said to be parts of one body. But I doubt if this is what it means. Paul of course uses the image of the body to stress the basic unity of Christians exercising various ministries in the community (1 Cor. 12.12–31). But he does this by explicitly and repeatedly affirming that 'All the members of the body though many are one body' (12.12). The hymn of the Rig-Veda does not do this. Its image suggests rather the hierarchical ranking of the four castes, and it has certainly been consistently understood in this way by Hindu tradition. The two creation myths thus reflect two different understandings of humankind. The *homo hierarchicus* of Hinduism stands over and against the *homo aequalis* of the Bible.[20]

The Bible's abstract affirmation of human dignity in primordial time is concretized by Jesus into a love ethic, whose basis is a new and profound insight into the biblical vision of the human person made in the image of God. As the image of God, the human person is understood in the creation story of the First Testament to be God's representative over creation, appointed to 'fill the earth and subdue it', and to 'have dominion over the birds of the air and over every living thing that moves upon the earth' (Gen. 1.28). Though this text has been misused to justify the technocratic exploitation of the world, this is surely not what the Bible has in mind. Humankind is to 'subdue the earth' as God's representative. That is, it must care for it with the same creative concern that God shows. The task of humankind is to foster creation; not to destroy it. The massive ecological destruction that we see around us is the work not of humankind playing out the role assigned to it in the Bible, but of a humankind that has abandoned the God of the Bible to become a worshipper of Mammon, who is indeed a callous, irresponsible and destructive god. Even in the anthropocentric world-view of the Bible, then, there is room to develop a bill of the rights of the cosmos, though this will always remain subordinate to the 'rights' of humankind.

But Jesus develops the metaphor of the human person as the image of God in a very different way. He sees this metaphor defining not so much the relationship of humankind to the cosmos as one person's relationship to another. If the human person has been created in the image of God, this, for Jesus, does not mean primarily that he or she is God's representative in the governing of creation. It means that he or she is God's sacrament in and through whom we get into touch with God. The basis of the ethics of Jesus is that our relationships with God are mediated through people. Humankind is the locus of our encounter with God.

This is expressed with great clarity in the love commandment in which Jesus sums up his ethic (Matt. 22.34–40). Here Jesus interprets the great commandment of Judaism, 'You shall love the Lord your God with all your heart and with all your soul and with all your might' (Deut. 6.5) by adding to it a not particularly significant injunction from the Holiness Code of Leviticus: 'You shall love your neighbour as yourself' (Lev. 19.18). This is more than a simple expansion of the Jewish command. The addition functions as an explanatory comment. Jesus here interprets Deut. 6.5 by means of Lev. 19.18. His great commandment therefore reads: 'You must love the Lord your God with all your heart, with all your soul, and with all your might; *this means*, that you must love your neighbour as yourself.' The love commandment of Jesus is, therefore, not that we love God *and* neighbour, as if these were two different objects of our love; but that we love God (the one object of our love) *by loving* our neighbour as we love ourselves. And the neighbour we are to love is understood by Jesus not in its First Testament sense of 'brother', or 'companion', or 'son of your own people' (Lev. 19.17–18), but in a wholly non-exclusive way as any one in need (Luke 10.29–37).

Just as we cannot love God except by loving neighbour, so too, Jesus tells us, we cannot be reconciled with God unless we are first reconciled with neighbour (Matt. 5.23–24). 'If you are offering your gift at the altar,' he says, 'and there remember that your neighbour has something against you, leave your gift there before the altar and go; first be reconciled to your neighbour and then come and offer your gift' (Matt. 5.23–24). The hilarious exaggeration of this 'case' can only be appreciated if we remember that the gift is being offered in the temple at Jerusalem, by someone who may have come from as far away as Galilee (where Jesus is speaking); and that the offence he or she has committed against this now distant neighbour is a trivial one (else it would not have been so completely forgotten). To ask this person to go back a three-day journey to be reconciled with the neighbour, before returning to offer his or her sacrifice, is not sensible advice. It is not meant to be. It is a hyberbolic overstatement to drive home as vividly as possible the point that Jesus wants to make, namely, that there is no way of being reconciled with God without being reconciled with one's fellow human beings. Right relations with God depend on right relationships with people.

That is why the New Testament does not quote Deut. 6.5 again, and speaks only rarely about our loving God. Instead it takes as its great commandment either Lev. 19.18, that we love our neighbour, understood in a wholly non-exclusive way, as much as we love ourselves (so Matt. 19.19; Rom. 13.8–10; Gal. 5.14; James 2.8); or, in the christological and sectarian language of John, that we love one another as Christ has loved us (John 13.34; 15.12). The great 'mantra' of the Christian faith is not 'I am brahman', but (if I might imitate the hyperbolic language of Jesus) 'You are god'. A human being, simply because he or she is human, confronts us as the image and the sacrament of God. The status that this gives the human person is the soundest basis one could imagine for human rights.

(b) Responsibility for the welfare of people: the basis of societal rights

This insight into the sacredness of the human person leads to a second biblical attitude, its insistence on our responsibility for the welfare people and specially of those in need. Such responsibility is based not only on the sacredness of people as individuals, but also, and indeed primarily, on the fact that God always relates to humankind (*ha'adam*) as a whole. The Bible affirms clearly the undivided solidarity of humankind, and so disallows Western individualism and the individualistic understanding of rights it has developed. It lays special stress on what we would call today social, economic and cultural rights, because it believes that serious responsibility for the welfare of people is implied in our solidarity with them. And it does this with unusual urgency because, being the literature of an oppressed people, it realizes how easily such responsibility can be shrugged off when the people for whom we are responsible are without power or voice.

Our responsibility for the well-being of people begins, then, with our solidarity with them in the oneness of humankind. This is affirmed in the opening pages of the Bible in the implied answer to the question of Cain: 'Am I my brother's keeper?' (Gen. 4.9). For the answer is, of course, 'Yes, you are!' A deeper awareness of this solidarity, and so a more compelling sense of our responsibility for others (but limited now to the covenant the community), develops with the emergence of Israel as a people. This finds expression in the law codes of the Pentateuch, with their conspicuous expressions of social concern for the poor of the people (Ex. 21.1–11; 22.21–27; Lev. 25.1–55; Deut. 15.1–18; 24.10–22); in the violent protests against injustice and exploitation that are an obsessive theme of the preaching of the prophets (see specially Isa. 3.13–15; 58.1–14; Amos 8.4–6; Micah 2.1–11); and above all in YHWH's repeated assertion that God is the protector of the powerless, that is, of 'the widow, the orphan and the refugee' (Deut. 10.17–19; 27.19; Jer. 22.3; Zech. 7.10).

The option for the powerless, explicitly made by YHWH, and demanded of YHWH's people (Ex. 22.21–24) and their king (Ps. 72.1–4; Isa. 11.4; Jer. 22.13–19), is reaffirmed by Jesus at a wholly new level of concern. Our responsibility for one another now becomes the overflow of God's love for us. It is this love which empowers us (I John 4.7) and is imaged by us (Matt. 5.45) when we do good to one another by responding effectively to one another's needs. The solidarity of humankind is, for Jesus, ultimately the solidarity of the 'family' created by God's love, in which God is experienced as parent and people as brothers and sisters. Such a solidarity obviously results in an altogether special sense of responsibility for the powerless. It is the kind of responsibility that Jesus himself demonstrated in his life and his teaching. For the life of Jesus was a progressive identification with the poor and the outcast (a journey from the centre to the periphery, as Kosuke Koyama has called it);[21] and in his teaching was the unchanging proclamation of the 'privilege of the poor', to whom alone the good news is preached (Luke 4.18–19; 7.22) and to whom alone God's rule belongs (Luke 6.20).

A growing awareness of our solidarity with humankind (as members of the human race, of the covenant people, of the family God), and an ever deepening sense of the responsibility that this solidarity implies, is what the Bible gives us. It is this that makes the Bible a charter for social economic and cultural rights.

Conclusion

As its foundation for human rights, the Bible offers us both an affirmation and a demand. While insisting on the inviolable sacredness of every human person it reminds us of the responsibility we have for one another, and specially for the rejected and the powerless of the world. Both affirmation and demand, implicit right and implicit duty, are part of the Bible's horizon. One does not exist without the other. We cannot ignore the Bible's teaching on human dignity, and attempt to base human rights on its 'covenant idea of co-responsibility' alone.[22] For in order to ground human rights, covenant co-responsibility must itself be grounded on a more basic value. Otherwise we may end up with a system like the caste hierarchy in India, which is justified precisely in terms of co-responsibility! The human rights covenants of the UN must indeed, as Aloysius Pieris observes, 'be subsumed within the frame of the biblical covenant (partnership between Yahweh and the weak) wherein *the obligations of the strong towards the weak* constitute the proper divine order'.[23] But this is only possible when we learn with the Bible to sense in the weak the sacredness of God.

Notes

1. Paul Sieghart, 'Christianity and Human Rights', *The Month* 150, 1989, 46–53:48; 51–3.

2. On the Western character of human rights, and the problems this poses for non-Western cultures, see Raimundo Panikkar, 'Is the Notion of Human Rights a Western Concept', *Diogenes* 120, 1982, 75–102; F. X. D'Sa, 'Das Recht, ein Mensch zu sein und die Pflicht, kosmisch zu bleiben', in Johannes Hoffmann (ed.), *Begründung von Menschenrechten aus der Sicht unterschiedlicher Kulturen*, Frankfurt 1981, 157–85.

3. George V. Lobo, *Human Rights in the Indian Context*, Delhi 1991, 5–11; Burns H. Weston, 'Human Rights', *The New Encyclopaedia Britannica*, Chicago [15]1974, Vol. 20, 714–22:714.

4. Sieghart, 'Christianity' (n. 1 above), 46.

5. Ibid., 47.

6. The Universal Declaration of Human Rights was adopted by the United Nations on 10 December 1948 as 'a common standard of achievement for all peoples and all nations' (Preamble). As such it is not legally binding, though it has acquired so great a moral authority that it serves as the conscience of the world. Its principles are embodied in two international covenants: on economic, social and cultural, and on civil and political rights, respectively. These were approved by the UN in 1966 and since 1976 have the binding force of lawful treaties on those nations who have ratified them. They have in fact been ratified by all the members of the UN except for the USA, the People's Republic of China and the Vatican!

7. David Hollenbach, *Claims in Conflict, Retrieving and Renewing the Catholic Human Rights Tradition*, New York 1979, 28.

8. Weston, 'Human Rights' (n. 3 above), 716–17.

9. Warren Lee Holleman, *The Human Rights Movement: Western Values and Theological Perspectives*, New York 1987, 85–7.

10. Weston, 'Human Rights' (n. 3 above), 717.

11. Richard A. Schweder, *Thinking Through Cultures, Expeditions in Cultural Psychology*, Cambridge, Mass. 1991, 153. Schweder is here speaking specifically about Indian society. But what he says is valid for other Third World societies as well. For as the anthropologist Clifford Geertz has pointed out, Western individualism is 'a rather peculiar idea within the context of the world's cultures' – quoted in Bruce Malina, *The*

New Testament World, Insights from Cultural Anthropology, Atlanta and London 1983, 54. We are talking here about cultural types, not about actual personalities, who, in any given culture, will approximate but never wholly conform to the dominant type. These types are moreover fluid, because cultures change as they interact with one another. Individualism is certainly increasing in the Third World with its growing modernity, and is likely to be the predominant type of the future.

12. Louis Dumont, *Homo Hierarchicus, the Caste System and Its Implications*, Delhi 1988, 4.

13. Schweder, *Thinking Through Cultures* (n. 11 above), 148–52.

14. Marvin Chaney, 'Ancient Palestinian Peasant Movements and the Formation of Premonarchic Israel', in David N. Freedman and David F. Graf (eds.), *Palestine in Transition: The Emergence of Ancient Israel*, Sheffield 1983, 39–90.

15. The ban was an ancient rite of the Holy War which at times may have been practised by Israel against a defeated enemy (I Sam. 15) or a recalcitrant city (Josh. 6.17), but never on the scale prescribed here. Here the language of the holy war is being used by the Deuteronomist to urge the destruction of Canaanite religion, then locked in a bitter struggle with Yahwism. The language is a significant indication of his attitude towards the Canaanites, and by extension to other Gentiles.

16. Sieghart, 'Christianity' (n. 1 above), 49.

17. I am not persuaded by the handful of universalistic texts collected by Werner Schmidt, *Alttestamentlicher Glaube in seiner Geschichte*, Neukirchen-Vluyn [7]1990, 319–24, to illustrate 'hope for the Gentiles'; nor by the poorly argued claim of Dennis McCarthy, 'Human Rights and the Old Testament', in Andrew Gonzalez (ed.), *Human Rights: A Christian Approach*, Manila 1988, 1–26, that though 'it might not centre on the idea, early on the Old Testament proclaims a divine concern for all men' [6]. There are a few texts in the First Testament which show YHWH's concern for 'the nations' but these do not alter its general anti-Gentile bias.

18. Gerhard von Rad, *Genesis*, London 1972, 60.

19. Ibid. Also, Hans Walter Wolff, *Anthropology of the Old Testament*, London 1974, 161–2.

20. The terms are from Louis Dumont, who entitled his classic work on the caste system *Homo hierarchicus* (Paris 1966) and followed this up with a study on Western society entitled *Homo aequalis* (Paris 1977).

21. Kosuke Koyama, 'Hallowed be Your Name', *IntRevMiss* 49, 1980/81, 280–2.

22. Aloysius Pieris, 'Three Inadequacies in the Social Encyclicals', *Vidyajoti* 57, 1993, 73–94:92.

23. Ibid., 93.

The Bible and the Preservation of the World

Norman Solomon

Introduction

The Second Vatican Council, in *Nostra Aetate* n. 4, spoke of the 'spiritual bonds linking' Jews and Christians, and of their 'great spiritual patrimony'. The 1985 *Notes on the Correct Way to Present the Jews and Judaism* affirmed the 'ongoing spiritual vitality' of Judaism. This article is offered, not as an enquiry into the 'ancient roots' of the Catholic faith, but as a contribution to the demonstration by living Jews and Catholics of the relevance of their common patrimony to a major contemporary issue.

We will examine the Bible (Hebrew Scriptures) as a source of those values that point to the preservation of the world as a human duty. Such values are sometimes perceived as 'humanistic'; their presence within a humanistic frame of reference in no way negates or undermines their status in biblical thought.

There are restraints on our reading. We do not leap direct from Bible to contemporary culture, but rather invite our religious tradition, of church or of synagogue, to mediate that journey. Therefore the Bible will be seen whole, in a faith context, rather than submitted to critical historical analysis.

The interpretation of Scripture which follows draws heavily on rabbinic tradition, which received its classical formulation in the Talmud, completed in Zoroastrian Babylonia in the sixth Christian century. This tradition still today unfolds in response to a changing world; it is expressed through *halakha* (law), history, myth, poetry and philosophy.

Attitudes to creation

Goodness of the physical world

'God saw that it was good' is the refrain of the first creation story in Genesis (1.1 to 2.4), which includes the physical creation of humankind, male and female. The created world is thus testimony to God's goodness and greatness (see Psalms 8; 104; 148; and Job 35.22–41.34).

The second 'creation' story (Genesis 2.5 to 3.24) accounts for the psychological make-up of humankind. Evil enters the world through the free exercise of choice by Adam and Eve, not in the process of creation, certainly not through fallen angels, devils, or any other external project of human guilt; such creatures are notably absent from the catalogue of creation in Genesis 1.

Post-biblical Judaism did not adopt the concept of 'the devil'. In the Middle Ages, however, the dualism of body and spirit prevailed, and with it a tendency to denigrate 'this world' and 'material things'. The Palestinian Kabbalist Isaac Luria (1534–1572) taught that God initiated the process of creation by 'withdrawing' himself from the infinite space he occupied; this theory stresses the 'inferiority' and distance from God of material creation, but compensates by drawing attention to the divine element concealed in all things.

Genesis 1 articulates 'original blessing' rather than 'original sin': 'God saw all that he had made, and it was very good' (Genesis 1.31) – and this includes all creatures, culminating with humans, female as well as male (Genesis 1.27).

Biodiversity

In Genesis 1 the Hebrew word *leminehu*, 'according to its kind', follows the names of most of the created items. The story of Noah's ark manifests anxiety that all species should be conserved, irrespective of their usefulness to humankind. There are careful lists and definitions of which species of creature might or might not be eaten (Leviticus 11 and Deuteronomy 14). Wool and linen are not to be mixed in a garment (Leviticus 19.19; Deuteronomy 22.11); ox and ass are not to plough together (Deuteronomy 22.10); fields (Leviticus 19.19) and vineyards (Deuteronomy 22.9) are not to be sown with mixed seeds or animals cross-bred (Leviticus 19.19); and, following the rabbinic interpretation of a thrice repeated biblical phrase (Exodus 23.19, 34.26; Deuteronomy 14.21), meat and milk may not be cooked or eaten together.

This biblical preoccupation with species and with keeping them distinct can now be read as a way of declaring the 'rightness' of God's pattern for creation and of calling on humankind not only not to interfere with it, but to cherish biodiversity by conserving species.

Scripture does not consider the evolution of species, with its postulates of (*a*) the alteration of species over time and (*b*) the extinction (long before the evolution of humans) of most species which have so far appeared on earth.[1] The Hebrew texts assign unique value to each species as it now is within the context of the present order of creation; this suffices to give a religious dimension, within Judaism, to the call to conserve species.

The wholeness of creation

Pereq shira[2] (the 'Chapter of Song') demonstrates Jewish affirmation of the wholeness of creation. This 'song' may have originated amongst the *hekhalot* mystics of the fourth or fifth centuries. By the twelfth century it featured prominently in private devotion. Its sections correspond to the physical creation (including heaven and hell, Leviathan and other sea creatures), plants and trees, creeping things, birds, and land animals. Each section consists of ten to twenty-five biblical verses, each interpreted as the song or saying of some part of creation or of some individual creature. The cock, in the fourth section, is given 'seven voices', and its function in the poem is to link the earthly song, in which all nature praises God, with the heavenly song. *Pereq shira* draws all creation, even the inanimate, even heaven and hell themselves, into the relationship, expressing a fullness which derives from the rich diversity in wholeness of God's creation.

Stewardship or domination?

The opening chapters of Genesis call on humans to act as stewards, guardians of creation. Adam was placed in the garden 'to till it and to care for it' (2.15). As Abraham Isaac Kook (1865–1935) put it:

No rational person can doubt that the Torah, when it commands people to 'rule over the fishes of the sea and the birds of the sky and all living things that move on the earth', does not have in mind a cruel ruler who exploits his people and servants for his own will and desires – God forbid that such a detestable law of slavery [be attributed to God] who 'is good to all and his tender care rests upon all his creatures' (Psalm 145.9) and 'the world is built on tender mercy' (Psalm 89.3).[3]

In the twelfth century the great Jewish Bible scholar Abraham ibn Ezra commented as follows on the words of Psalm 115.16: 'The heavens are the heavens of the Lord, and he gave the earth to people.'

The ignorant have compared man's rule over the earth with God's rule over the heavens. This is not right, for God rules over everything. The meaning of 'he gave it to people' is that man is God's steward (*paqid* – officer with responsibility for a specific task) over the earth, and must do everything according to God's word.

It is perverse to understand 'and rule over it' (Genesis 1.28) – let alone Psalm 8 – as meaning 'exploit and destroy' (is that what people think of their rulers?). The context of Genesis 1.28 is that of humans being made in the image of God, the beneficent creator of good things; its meaning is therefore very precise, that humans, being in the image of God, are summoned to share in his creative work, and to do all in their power to *sustain* creation.

Hierarchy in creation

'God created humans in his image . . . male and female he created them' (Genesis 1.27). Humankind, created on the sixth day, is superior to animals, animals to plants, plants to the inanimate. There is a *hierarchy* in created things.

The hierarchical model has two practical consequences. First is that of responsibility of the higher for the lower, traditionally expressed as 'rule', latterly as 'stewardship'. The second is that, in a competitive situation, the higher has priority over the lower. If I am driving my car and find myself unable to avoid hitting either a dog or a child I would undoubtedly choose to hit the dog.

Is it right to take a human life, e.g. that of a poacher, to save not an individual animal but an endangered species? Nothing in Jewish sources supports killing poachers in any circumstances other than those in which they directly threaten human life. Even if homicide were justified in such circumstances, how many human lives is a single species worth? How far down the evolutionary scale would such a principle be applied? To microscopic species? Plants?

Torah, consistently with the hierarchical principle of creation, values human life more than that of other living things, but at the same time stresses the special responsibility of human beings 'to till . . . and to care for' the created order.

The Spanish Jewish philosopher Joseph Albo (1380–1435) places humans at the top of the earthly hierarchy, and discerns in this the possibility for humans to receive God's revelation.[4] God's revelation, *pace* Albo and Jewish tradition, is the Torah, from which we learn our responsibilities towards each other and towards the rest of creation. The superiority of humans lies in their unique combination of freedom to choose and the intelligence to judge, without which the divine revelation would have no application. Being in this sense 'higher' than other creatures, humans must be humble towards all. Albo, in citing these passages and commending the reading of *Pereq shira* (see above), articulates the attitude of humble stewardship towards creation which characterizes rabbinic Judaism.

Concern for animals

Kindness to animals is a motivating factor for general concern with the environment, rather than itself an element in conservation. It features prominently in the Jewish tradition. The Ten Commandments include domestic animals in the Sabbath rest, and the 'seven Noahide laws' are even more explicit.[5] Pious tales and folklore exemplify this attitude, as in the Talmudic anecdote of rabbi Judah the Patriarch's contrition over having sent a calf to the slaughter.[6]

This concern condenses into the concept of *tsaar baalei hayyim* ('distress to living creatures'). The third-century Babylonian, Rav, ruled that one should feed one's cattle before breaking bread oneself;[7] even the Sabbath laws are relaxed somewhat to enable rescue of injured animals or milking of cows to ease their distress. Recently, concern has been expressed about intensive animal husbandry including battery chicken production; rabbinic responsa have appeared on the restraints to be placed on experimentation on animals. Experimentation is not allowed for frivolous purposes; it is necessary to define both the human benefits which might justify animal experimentation and the safeguards necessary to avoid unnecessary suffering to animals.[8]

The Torah does not enjoin vegetarianism, though Adam and Eve were vegetarian (Genesis 1.19). Restrictions on meat-eating perhaps indicate reservations. Albo wrote that the first people were forbidden to eat meat because of the cruelty involved in killing animals; this was endorsed by Isaac Abravanel (1437–1508), who taught that when the Messiah comes we would return to the ideal, vegetarian state.[9] Today the popular trend to vegetarianism has won many Jewish adherents, though little official backing from religious leaders.[10]

Jewish tradition despises hunting for sport, as witness the strong censure voices by Ezekiel Landau (1713–93), rabbi of Prague.[11] The grounds for objection are ethical and ritual rather than conservationist.

The land and the people – a paradigm

Judaism developed within a specific context of peoplehood. The Bible emphasizes the inter-relationship of people and land, the idea that the prosperity of the land depends on the people's obedience to God's covenant:

> If you pay heed to the commandments which I give you this day, and love the Lord your God and serve him with all your heart and soul, then I will send rain for your land in season . . . and you will gather your corn and new wine and oil, and I will provide pasture . . . you shall eat your fill. Take good care not to be led astray in your hearts nor to turn aside and serve other gods . . . or the Lord will become angry with you; he will shut up the skies and there will be no rain, your ground will not yield its harvest, and you will soon vanish from the rich land which the Lord is giving you (Deuteronomy 11.13–17).

Two steps are required to apply this link between morality and prosperity to the contemporary situation:

1. The chosen land and people must be understood as the prototype of (a) all actual individual geographical nations (including, of course, Israel) in their relationships with land and of (b) humanity as a whole in its relationship with the planet as a whole.

2. There must be satisfactory clarification of the meaning of 'obedience to God' as the human side of the covenant to ensure that 'the land will be blessed'. The Bible certainly has in mind justice and moral rectitude, but in spelling out 'the commandments of God' it includes specific prescriptions which directly regulate care of the land and celebration of its produce.

In sum, the Bible stresses the intimate relationship between people and land. The prosperity of land depends on (a) the social justice and moral integrity of the people on it and (b) a caring, even loving, attitude to land with effective regulation of its use. Conservation demands the extrapolation of these principles from ancient or idealized Israel to the contemporary global situation; this calls for education in social values together with scientific investigation of the effects of our activities on nature.

Sabbatical year and jubilee

> When you enter the land which I give you, the land shall keep sabbaths to the Lord. For six years you may sow your fields and for six years prune your vineyards but in the seventh year the land shall keep a sabbath of sacred rest, a sabbath to the Lord. You shall not sow your field nor prune your vineyard . . . (Leviticus 25.2–4).

The analogy between the sabbath ('rest day') of the land and that of people signifies that land must 'rest' to be refreshed and regain its productive vigour. That is, land resources must be conserved through the avoidance of over-use.

The Bible pointedly links this to social justice. Just as land must not be exploited, so slaves must go free after six years of bondage or in the jubilee (fiftieth) year, and the sabbatical year (in Hebrew *shemitta* – 'release') cancels private debts, thus preventing exploitation of the individual.

The consequence of disobedience is exile from the land, which God so cares for that he will heal it in the absence of its unfaithful inhabitants.

> If in spite of this you do not listen to me and still defy me . . . I will make your cities desolate and destroy your sanctuaries . . . your land shall be desolate and your cities heaps of rubble. Then, all the time that it lies desolate, while you are in exile in the land of your enemies, your land shall enjoy its sabbaths to the full . . . (Leviticus 26.27–35).

The biblical text has undoubtedly influenced scientists and agronomists in Israel today to question the intensive agriculture favoured in the early years of the state and to give high priority to conservation of land resources.

Cutting down fruit trees

> When you are at war, and lay siege to a city . . . do not destroy its trees by taking the axe to them, for they provide you with food . . . (Deuteronomy 20.19).

In its biblical context this is a counsel of prudence rather than a principle of conservation; the Israelites are enjoined to use only 'non-productive', that is, non fruit-bearing trees, for their siege works.

In rabbinic teaching the verse has become the *locus classicus* for conserving all that has been created. The very phrase *bal tashchit*[12] is inculcated into small children to teach them not to destroy or waste even those things they do not need. Rabbi Aaron Halevi of Barcelona (c. 1300) explained:

> This is meant to ingrain in us the love of that which is good and beneficial and to cleave to it; by this means good will imbue our souls and we will keep far from everything evil or destructive. This is the way of the devout and those of good deeds – they love peace, rejoice in that which benefits people and brings them to Torah; they never destroy even a grain of mustard, and are upset at any destruction they see. If only they can save anything from being spoilt they spare no effort to do so.[13]

Mishna prohibits the use of olive and fig wood on the altar; Aha bar Jacob maintained that this was because the destruction of such trees would frustrate settlement of the land.[14]

Limitation of grazing rights

Mishna (*Bava Qama* 7.7) rules: 'One may not raise small cattle[15] in the land of Israel, but one may do so in Syria or in the uninhabited parts of the land of Israel.' Later rabbis suggest that the primary purpose of the law is to prevent the 'robbery' of crops by roaming animals; alternatively, its objective is to encourage settlement in the land. This latter reason is based on the premise that the raising of sheep and goats is inimical to the cultivation of crops, and reflects the ancient rivalry between nomad and farmer; at the same time it poses the question considered by modern ecologists of whether animal husbandry is an efficient way of producing food.

Agricultural festivals

The concept of 'promised land' is an assertion that the consummation of social and national life depends on harmony with the land.

The biblical pilgrim-festivals all celebrate the land and its crops, though they are also given historical and spiritual meanings. Through the joyful collective experience of these festivals the people learned to cherish the land and their relationship, through God's commandments, with it; the sense of joy was heightened through fulfilment of the divine commandments to share the bounty of the land with 'the Levite, the stranger, the orphan and the widow' (Deuteronomy 16.11 and elsewhere).

Other environmental laws

Arising from Deuteronomy 23.13,14 *halakha* insists that refuse be removed 'outside the camp', that is, collected in a location where it will not degrade the quality of life. Talmud and codes extend this concept to the general prohibition of dumping refuse or garbage where it may interfere with the environment or with crops.

Smell is regarded as a particular nuisance; hence there are rules regarding the siting not only of lavatories but also of odoriferous commercial operations such as tanneries.[16] Clearly, rabbinic law accords priority to environmental over purely commercial considerations.

Like smell, atmospheric pollution and smoke are placed by the rabbis within the category of indirect damage, since their effects are produced at a distance. They are nevertheless unequivocally forbidden.

Mishna (*Bava Batra* 2) bans the siting of a threshing floor within fifty cubits of a residential area, since the flying particles set in motion by the threshing process would diminish the quality of the air. Likewise (*Bava Batra* 1.7), a furnace may not be sited within fifty cubits of a residential area because of the effect of its smoke on the atmosphere; the fifty-cubit limit was subsequently extended by the Gaonim to whatever the distance from which smoke might cause eye irritation or general annoyance.[17]

Several laws were instituted by the rabbis to safeguard the freedom from pollution (as well as the fair distribution) of water.

Mishna lays down that in a residential area neighbours have the right to object to the opening of a shop or similar enterprise on the grounds that the noise would disturb their tranquillity. It is permitted, however, to open a school for Torah notwithstanding the noise of children, for education has priority (*Hoshen Mishpat* 156.3).

Rabbinic legislation to enhance the environment is rooted in the biblical law of the Levitical cities (Leviticus 35.2–5). As this passage is understood by the rabbis, there was to be a double surround to each town, first a 'green belt' of a thousand cubits, then a two thousand cubit wide belt for 'fields and vineyards'.

The rabbinic appreciation of beauty in nature is illustrated in the blessing to be recited when one sees 'the first blossoms in Spring':

> You are blessed, Lord our God and ruler of the universe, who have omitted nothing from your world, but created within it good creatures and good and beautiful trees in which people may take delight.[18]

Procreation versus population control

The world cannot be preserved unless its human population is kept within bounds. Medical science and enhanced food production have allowed the human population to increase but, as Malthus remarked, population if unchecked grows exponentially, food resources only arithmetically.

Judaism permits some forms of birth control where a potential mother's life is in danger; abortion is not only permissible but mandatory up to full term to save the mother's life.[19] Though contraception is morally questionable, it is preferable to abstinence where danger to life would be involved through normal sexual relations within marriage.[20]

What happens where economic considerations rather than danger to life come into play? When Resh Lakish (third century) ruled, 'It is forbidden to engage in sexual intercourse in years of famine' (BT *Taanit* 11a), he had in mind only local or temporary famine, not the upward pressure of population on finite world resources. Indeed, that concept was unknown to the classical sources of the Jewish religion. As the duty of procreation is expressed in Genesis in the words 'be fruitful and multiply and fill the earth', one might suggest that 'fill' be taken as 'reach the maximum population sustainable at an acceptable standard of living but do not exceed it'. The rabbis themselves (BT *Yevamot* 62a) utilized Isaiah's phrase 'God made the earth . . . no empty void, but made it for a place to dwell in' (45.18) to define the minimum requirement for procreation – a requirement, namely one son and one daughter, which does not increase population.

Conclusion. The Bible as cultural heritage

In conclusion, we affirm that the Bible, our common cultural heritage, promotes a conservationist ideology.

First, Genesis' declaration of the primal goodness of creation and of the human duty to 'till and preserve' it, orientates us towards conservation.

Then, when we read the Bible as the story of people and land, we discover that biblical laws carry 'conservationist' messages: the sabbatical year teaches us not to overuse land, the laws on mixtures teach us respect for biodiversity. The cycle of festivals is a prototype public educational programme instilling respect for nature.

Tradition models specific legislation for pollution control of air, water, and environment and the diminution of nuisances such as noise and smell.

However, we must not ask too much. We may draw inspiration from the past, but we cannot obtain precise answers. It would be anachronistic to seek in the earlier sources the concept of waste disposal as threatening the total balance of nature or the climate. However, if the rabbis forbade the growing of kitchen gardens and orchards around Jerusalem on the grounds that the manuring would degrade the local environment,[21] we follow hard on their heels in showing deep concern at the large-scale environmental degradation caused by traditional mining operations, or the burning of fossil fuels.

'Having the Bible on our side' in espousing conservation transforms what would be mere issues of prudence into questions of love, into respect for the awe and majesty of God's creation. That is precisely the point of rooting 'humanistic' values in biblical tradition.

Notes

1. To the third-century Palestinian Rabbi Abbahu the Midrash *Bereshit Rabbah* 3.9 attributes the statement that God 'created and destroyed worlds before he made this' – his final perfect design.

2. Texts (Hebrew) are in the Prayer Books of Jacob Emden and Seligmann Baer.

3. Cited from the texts on *Protection of Animals*, ed. N. Rakover for the Israel Ministry of Justice, Jerusalem 1976.

4. Joseph Albo, *Sefer Ha-Iqqarim*, book III, Chapter 1 (English version *Book of Principles*, ed. I. Husik, Philadelphia 1946).

5. The 'Seven Laws of the Children of Noah' attempt to define the religious obligations of humankind in general, for all people are descended from Noah. The laws, unknown in this form in sources earlier than the third century, are: Do not blaspheme, do not worship idols, do not murder, do not commit adultery, do not steal, do establish courts of justice, do not eat 'a limb torn from a living animal'. The last of these covers cruelty to animals.

6. BT (Babylonian Talmud) *Bava Metzia* 85a.

7. BT *Berakhot* 20a and *Orah Hayyim* 167.6.

8. See Elijah Judah Shochet, *Animal Life in Jewish Tradition: Attitudes and Relationships*, New York 1984, and J. David Bleich, *Contemporary Halakhic Problems*, vol. 3, New York 1989, 194–236 for the halakhic literature on these themes.

9. Albo, *Sefer Ha-Iqqirim* (n. 4), 3.15; Isaac Abravanel, *Commentary* on Isaiah 11 and Genesis 2.

10. See Richard Schwarz, *Judaism and Vegetarianism*, New York 1982, and Bleich, *Halakhic Problems* (n. 8), 237–250b.

11. Ezekiel Landau, *Noda biYehuda*, Vol. 2, *Yore Deah* 10.

12. Literally 'not to destroy'. In BT *Makkot* 22a Ravina (fourth century) stresses the positive aspect of the commandment, 'but you shall eat (the fruit of the trees)'.

13. *Sefer Ha-Hinnukh, Mitzva* 529.

14. Mishna *Tamid* 2.3 (BT 29b); cf. Mishna *Shevi'it*, end of no. 4.

15. Sheep and goats.

16. BT *Bava Batra* no. 2; *Hoshen Mishpat* 145.

17. The Gaonim were the heads of Babylonian academies in the sixth to tenth centuries; they played a major role in the transmission and development of rabbinic law.

18. Judah bar Exekiel (third-century Palestinian) in BT *Berakhot* 43b.

19. See David M. Feldman, *Marital Relations, Birth Control and Abortion in Jewish Law*, New York 1974.

20. Ibid., 302.

21. BT *Bava Oama* 82b.

'Behold I Make All Things New': The Final Statement of the Fourth Plenary Assembly of the Catholic Biblical Federation

Teresa Okure

The Catholic Biblical Federation held its fourth plenary, six-yearly, assembly in Bogota, Colombia, in 1990. The theme of the assembly was 'The Bible and the New Evangelization'. The key biblical text adopted for the assembly was 'Behold, I make all things new' (Isa. 43.19; Rev. 21.5).[1] The Final Statement of the assembly mapped out the course which the Catholic Biblical Federation was to follow after the assembly in order to carry out the aims of its twenty-one years of existence,[2] namely, 'to serve the bishops in their pastoral responsibilities concerning the wider use and knowledge of the Bible', in particular, to 'implement the very important goals set forth in chapter VI of the Second Vatican Council's Constitution on Divine Revelation'.[3] As the Final Statement notes, 'the Plenary Assembly coincided with the twenty-fifth anniversary of the promulgation of *Dei Verbum*, the Vatican II Constitution on Divine Revelation',[4] a document which inspired the formation of the Catholic Biblical Federation.

This article offers an extensive review and critical evaluation of the Final Statement. It also highlights other implications of the key biblical text which the Catholic Biblical Federation chose for the theme of its assembly. It comes within the general framework of the concern to highlight the mutual influence between cultures and the Bible with special focus on how the Bible should advance pastoral ministries in multi-cultural and cross-cultural contexts.

Content of the Final Statement

The Final Statement, a 21-page document, has five parts, with an introduction and a conclusion. The introduction gives the date, venue, theme and number of participants at the assembly. An impressive number of 140 participants, including delegates and observers from 70 countries and 5 continents, took part in it (1.1). This gives an average of 2 and 28 participants from each of the participating countries and continents, respectively.

Part One: The Call for a New Evangelization. The impetus for the theme of the Assembly, 'The Bible and the New Evangelization', is located in the call of Pope John Paul II for a 'new evangelization in the whole world as we move into the third millennium' (2.1). The Bible plays a key role in this task. The Assembly noted 'the great changes and newness' which are currently taking place in the world and in the church (2.2, a-g). All these changes in areas such as science and technology, media and computer revolution, ecology, the re-emergence of ancient and 'Third World' cultures, women's issues, the phenomenon of fundamentalism and the politics of new Eastern Europe, are said to cause 'the emergence of a totally new world order which is beyond our expectations' (2.2).

The church, whose primary task is evangelization, finds 'herself in the midst of this newness, challenged to a new evangelization in response to the newness around her'. This call for a new evangelization is traced back to the Second Vatican Council, which, in the vision of John XXIII, is described as 'the new Pentecost . . . in the Church of our days', and to *Evangelii Nuntiandi* (1975) of Paul VI, which first spoke of the 'new era of evangelization' (2.3).

While there is this emphasis on new evangelization, the Final Statement rightly admits that this 'newness' is inherent in evangelization itself, because 'it is the saving work of the Lord Jesus himself' in whom 'God has made all things new'. Because Christian evangelization 'is always [and by nature] new', the newness for us today, as for past and future generations, consists in discovering 'anew the newness of the Gospel message' (2.4) as it applies to our own contexts.

Next, the Final Statement addresses the Latin American context in which the assembly took place. The 500th anniversary of Christian evangelization in this continent gives a composite picture of the good and the bad in evangelization. The good lies in the faith and self-sacrifice of genuine missionaries who gave authentic witness to the love of Christ in their proclamation of the gospel. The bad lies in the way in which some Christians compromised their testimony by 'political and economic interests', 'through their unjust exploitation of the riches of this land as well as through their lack of respect for the human rights of the people who lived there for centuries' (3.1; 3.2).

Section 4 discusses the relation between the new evangelization (4.1) and the biblical apostolate (4.2) and highlights the role of the Catholic Biblical Federation in the new evangelization (4.3). The new evangelization is a task which belongs to 'the whole Church; from the head to the members, at both the universal and local levels'. The task also touches upon every aspect of the church's life: 'kerygmatic proclamation, catechesis, liturgical celebration, service to the world, theological reflection, pastoral practice and institutional structures'.

As an important aspect of the new evangelization, biblical apostolate seeks to ensure that '"All the preaching of the Church, like the Christian religion itself"' is '"nourished and directed by the Holy Scriptures" (DV 21)' (4.2). The basic concern of the Catholic Biblical Federation, then, is 'to make sure that the Bible takes its rightful place in this project of the universal Church at different levels and in different regions, to identify how the Bible can best be used to promote it, and what the Federation can do to act to promote and support such endeavours'. The journey of the Catholic Biblical Federation in its plenary assemblies from Vienna (1972) though Malta (1978) and Bangalore (1984) to Bogota (1990) is seen as 'a gradual build-up under the inspiration of the Holy Spirit, of an organized biblical-pastoral response to the challenges of the new evangelization' (4.3).

Part Two: What Is Understood by the New Evangelization. The understanding of the new evangelization is now rooted in a trinitarian framework: 'God is present in life, in nature and in history (Pss. 8.1–10; 19.2–7), since everything was created in Christ and for Christ (Col. 1.15–18). The Spirit of Christ is at work in all humanity, leading it towards Christ through different paths and gifts (cf. John 14.2).' This awareness demands that 'we listen to the living Word that God speaks in order to be able to proclaim it (DV 1)' (5.1).

This affirmation is followed by the recognition that like the disciples on the road to Emmaus (Luke 24.13–35), we 'sometimes still do not perceive the presence of Christ, who walks with us (Luke 24,16)', and that unlike Paul, 'we are not always able to recognize within them [the history of peoples] the presence of Christ'. This recognition calls for an evangelization that will be 'new' in its ardour, its methods, and its expressions (5.2; 5.3).[5]

This 'newness' in methods and expressions of evangelization requires that the evangelizers first allow themselves to be evangelized, that is, 'feel the challenge and the crises of the newness', 'go through the darkness and the experience of not knowing', and 'experience the temptation of following other paths'. Through this 'radical obedience' they come 'in a new and gratuitous way', to experience 'the friendly face of God who makes life arise from death' and 'that Jesus is the Lord' (5.4). This new experience of God gives the evangelizers 'new eyes' to understand God's action in the past, and with this insight they are able to 'discern the signs of the Reign of God which is coming about in the life and history of our peoples' (5.5). The evangelized evangelizers then become open to the Spirit of God who enables them to understand the Word which God addresses to them, and who equips them to be witnesses to the ends of the earth, and to evangelize as the first disciples did in the Acts of the Apostles: such as Peter (Acts 2.14–36; 3.11–26), Philip (8.26–40), Paul (17.22–31; Eph. 1.9–19; I Cor. 15.28), and the community at Antioch (Acts 11.19–26). It will include denouncing 'like Paul before Peter what is wrong in the Church itself (Gal. 2.14)'. The whole undertaking aims at enabling all to 'have life, and have it to the full' (John 10.10), in a system where God is all in all (I Cor. 15.25) (5.6).

This 'new experience of God in Jesus Christ' also gives birth to a new courage which leads the evangelizer to speak out boldly and choose to obey God rather than human beings (Acts 4.19–20). The new ardour becomes 'a force and a light that will help us be the leaven of a new humanity (Matt. 13.33)', 'the guarantee of a new heaven and a new earth (Isa. 65,17)'. It forces the evangelizer to 'announce the Good News of the Reign of God in the same way as Jesus did on the way to Emmaus' (5.7).

Section 5.8–16 explores as a pardigm the pedagogy which Jesus uses in proclaiming the message to the disciples on the road to Emmaus (Luke 24.13–35). Central to this pedagogy is that Jesus listens to the disciples in what they believe to be a hopeless situation (5.8); he accompanies them as a friend and dialogues with them (5.9). This listening, dialoguing attitude is seen as the first step in the new evangelization, one which also led Jesus to spend thirty years in the humble home in Nazareth 'in order to learn what to announce during the three years of public life' (5.10).

The second step in the new pedagogy is to help the disciples, in a process of guided discovery, to read events with new eyes. By going through what they already know, namely their scriptures, Jesus helps them to reinterpret these known scriptures 'in the light of his Resurrection' and thus 'clarifies the situation in which the disciples found themselves' (5.11). The wisdom of the pedagogy lies in that 'the new' which Jesus proclaims 'is not totally new', but is 'an ancient newness that is found in the history and in the hope of the people'. By reading the scriptures thus, Jesus 'breaks the erroneous vision of the dominant ideology and helps the disciples to discover the presence of God' (5.12). Moreover, by placing 'the event, the cross, within the broader perspective of God's design', he helps them to 'discover that they are not lost' and that 'the history of the world continues in the hands of God' (5.13).

In sum, Jesus interprets the scriptures by starting with 'the concrete problem of the disciples, and discovers in the situation new criteria for listening to the texts'. He uses the scriptures to give 'light to the situation' and open 'a horizon of hope'. In the process he helps the disciples to 'perceive the mistakes and calls for conversion' (5.14).

It is noted that 'the scriptures by themselves do not necessary give new sight'. They 'barely make our hearts burn inside (Luke 24.32)'. The 'new eyes' is given in the third step of new evangelization, namely, in 'the concrete gesture of sharing (Luke 24.31)' that makes one perceive the presence of the risen Christ (Luke 24.31). This gesture of sharing gives birth to a community in which 'Christians have all in common (Acts 2.44–45; 4.32–35)'. The eucharist constitutes 'the highest expression of this communion' and 'reveals the sacramental dimension of the Word of God' (5.15). By discovering the presence of the risen Christ within community, the disciples themselves 'are risen and are reborn'; they discover in cross and death the 'sign of life and hope' and the 'root of freedom and courage' (5.16). In short, the new pedagogy of which the episode of Emmaus forms a paradigm leads to the experience of true 'conversion which is transforming reality, creating new ways of human living together' (5.17).

Part Three: How the New Evangelization Becomes Good News. This section of the Final Statement underlines that for the new evangelization to become good news it needs to become aware of the 'different and specific life contexts' of peoples as the *loci* where they are to experience salvation. The specific contexts listed and commented upon include the context of cultural pluralism (6.1), the context of socio-political and economic situation (6.2), the contexts of ecological imbalances (6.3), of multi-religious situations (6.4), of people emerging from totalitarian systems (6.5), of the new awakening of marginalized peoples on the basis of ethnic, linguistic, economic, social, sexist or political reasons (6.6), of ecumenism (6.7), and of Christian communities (6.8).

Each of these contexts calls for its own distinctive approach to evangelization. That of cultural pluralism, for instance, calls for the approach of inculturation, while that of ecological imbalances calls for a 'balanced view' where current 'human greed' will give way to 'human need' in the use of earth's resources, and where all will join forces with the young and women in caring for creation instead of exploiting it. It also requires a critical re-reading of Gen. 1–11 alongside other biblical texts (Job 38–39; Ps. 104; Prov. 8.22–31) which give a decentralized view of human beings in God's plan. The context of multi-religious situations where people reclaim their right to practise their religion often in a fundamentalist way calls for a move by Christians from apologetics to dialogue, while safeguarding their own right to proclaim the gospel and to criticize tendencies in religions to violate human rights and human values. It also leads to efforts to build the world together, even if it is impossible to have a community of faith.

Aware that not all the current ways of reading the Bible are equally apt, the Final Statement spells out new ways of reading the Bible to meet the needs of the different contexts. Significantly, the Final Statement recommends beginning with the actual living situation as the place where God speaks the word through the Bible, the church and the human situation. In this way one learns to see God concretely, rather than philosophically, present in human lives (7.2). Prayerful reading opens us to God's self-communication in love which is the main purpose of his speaking to us (7.2). The reading should also seek to discover the true content of the Bible and should eschew all ideological or political readings which are a betrayal of the message (7.3). To avoid the danger of fundamentalism, the Bible is to be read in the context of the believing community and within its own socio-historical contexts. Note is to be taken of the progressive nature of biblical revelation which culminates in Christ, and the existence of the many literary forms is to be recognized (7.4). This new reading thus gives rise to a new biblical apostolate (7.5).

Part Four: Practical Recommendations. The Final Statement ends with practical recommendations aimed at promoting the required and desired biblical apostolate in order 'to ensure that the Bible is not only possessed and read but also believed and lived' (8). These recommendations are directed to 'the whole Church' (8.1, 1–2), to the Catholic Biblical Foundation (8.2, 1–3), and to its members (8.3, 1–6), each with its own sub-sections). Some of the most innovative aspects as well as the greatest weaknesses of the Final Statement appear in this section. The recommendations are very extensive, clearly set out, but somewhat ambitious. For practical reasons, I shall discuss some of them in the next part of this article, which is the evaluation of the document.

Critical evaluation of the Final Statement

When the Final Statement appeared four years ago, it was in many ways an innovative document of the church. Here I can only highlight some of its high and weak points.[6] On the positive side, its contents convey very well the conviction of the Federation that the Bible should be made to address every aspect of human life: religious, political, ecumenical, inter-faith, ecological, economic, social and so forth. This arises from the firm belief in the inherent power of the Bible as the Word of God to address, challenge and transform these human situations. The Bible is seen as 'the Book for the world', which cannot be understood 'without the human reality in need of salvation, nor can we understand the human reality without the Bible' (6.2). This is because the same God who speaks in the Bible and decisively through Christ (Heb. 1.1–2), through whom God created all things and to whom the scriptures bear witness (John 5.39), is also present and active in the lives of peoples and their cultures. Because of this truth, it needs to be added that we cannot fully understand the mystery of Jesus himself, the Word made flesh, without the human reality in need of salvation. Not only the Bible, then, but also the whole of theology and christology need to be grounded in the human reality for their authentic and proper comprehension.

Another laudable aspect of the Final Statement is the call for a new approach or orientation in the interpretation of scripture. This interpretation is to be put at the service of the pastoral ministry of the church, that is, at the service of concrete lives of peoples in their different social and cultural locations and existential situations. This is why 'inculturation of the gospel message' is seen as the 'necessary condition for any meaningful ministry of the Word', because among other things, it helps to 'unfold the riches of the gospel' (6.1). The use of the story of Jesus' encounter with the disciples on the road to Emmaus offers a good example of the kind of re-reading which the document advocates.

A corollary of this is the assertion that the actual situation in which peoples live should furnish the criteria for the interpretation of scripture. This means, too, that each of the different contexts of peoples of the world listed in Section 6 should furnish its own criteria for interpreting the Bible. This is in keeping with the method which Jesus himself used in proclaiming the reign of God. His many parables, for instance, testify to his ability to adapt his teaching to his different audiences, using their common traditions and particular human situations. This insight of the document means that as the Bible enriches people's life-situations by shedding light on them, challenging them and bringing transforming hope, even so the Bible itself is enriched by these multi-cultural contexts in which it is interpreted. This, as I have noted elsewhere, is one of the rich blessings which inculturation brings to the proclamation of the gospel and to the entire life of the church.[7] Similar blessings come from listening to the gospel which the poor and 'oppressed peoples preach to us' (6.6).

The Final Statement is also right in stating that not all current methods of interpretation of the Bible are equally apt. This position finds strong support in the recent publication of the Pontifical Biblical Commission, *The Interpretation of Scripture in the Church*.[8] This new document gives a panoramic description and critical assessment of current methods of interpreting the Bible. It has, for instance, the same strong reservation as does the Final Statement, about the fundamentalist interpretation of scripture which both documents describe as 'dangerous'.[9] Both the Final Statement and *The Interpretation* agree on the importance of allowing the Bible to address the concrete situations in which people live.[10] The influence of 'Third World' theologies is clearly manifest in this stance of both documents.

Another important feature of the Final Statement worth noting is the emphasis on the need for the evangelizers themselves to become evangelized or converted, and the open admission of past mistakes as a necessary condition for becoming effective agents of the Good News to others. Equally noteworthy is the recognition of the need for courage and boldness on the part of the evangelizers not only to proclaim the word fearlessly as the apostles did (Acts 4.19–20; Final Statement 5.7) and denounce what is wrong in peoples' religions and cultures (Acts 7.1–54; 14.11–18; Final Statement 5.5) but to challenge and denounce what is wrong within the church itself, with regard to its structures and practices, following the example of Paul *vis-à-vis* Peter at Antioch (Gal. 2.14; Final Statement 5.5).

On the weak side, the Final Statement as a document is very expansive, somewhat repetitive and generally difficult to follow. One example of the diffuseness which generates confusion is in the use of the term 'new'. The goal envisaged by the Final Statement is the establishment of the 'new heaven and new earth'. All its statements and recommendations aim at this. Hence the document frequently speaks of 'new' and 'newness' in a variety of ways: 'new eyes', 'new ways', 'new challenges', 'new paths', 'new methods', 'new experience of God', 'new evangelization', 'newness around us'. But the meanings of 'newness' in each of these references do not function at the same level. For instance, it is doubtful that 'the great newness and changes' mentioned in 2.1, 2.2 are necessarily evidence of the coming of the 'new heaven and new earth' (Final Statement 5.7) which is the goal of the biblical-pastoral apostolate of the Catholic Biblical Federation. The key biblical texts cited in the Final Statement, Isa. 43.19; 65.17; Rev. 21.5, need to be read in their own socio-historical contexts for an accurate assessment of the value of these 'newness and changes' which are taking place in the church in the world.

It is obvious that the Catholic Biblical Federation considers this Final Statement to be a very important document because of the cosmic nature of the issues raised in it and the scope of activities involved. One of the greatest challenges of the document is that of implementation. Several issues of the *Bulletin Dei Verbum* which appeared after the Bogota assembly give account of how the members of the Federation are implementing the decisions of the assembly in their different countries.[11] Yet four years after the assembly, most people outside the membership of Catholic Biblical Federation do not know of the existence of the document, as I found out in trying to locate it for the purposes of this study. The challenge of implementation is closely linked with that of circulation. For the document to achieve maximum success, it will need to be made available to as many as possible of the envisaged agents of implementation, e.g. theological institutions, houses of formation and seminaries, not just to bishops and the members of the Catholic Biblical Federation.

The Final Statement also contains a certain ambivalence worth noting. On the one hand it emphasizes that the 'new evangelization' is the task and concern of 'the whole church' (4.1), and that the new thrust of the biblical-pastoral apostolate should be 'a thrust from institutional structure to creative presence' and from 'clergy to laity' (7.5.2–3). Yet the first set of recommendations made 'to the whole Church' (8.1.1–3) is addressed only to 'Bishops and Bishops' Conferences'. Understandably, this is the body that can appoint the recommended 'Bible Sundays, weeks, months or even a Bible year' (8.1.2), or ask that a Synod of Bishops be dedicated to the 'Biblical-Pastoral Ministry' (8.1.2). Still, this section leaves one with the impression that 'the whole Church' is synonymous with bishops and episcopal conferences. This is clearly not true in the biblical/gospel perspective and in that of *Lumen Gentium* (especially chapter 2).

Another aspect of the ambivalence is that in mentioning changes in the world, the Final Statement says very little, if anything, about actual changes in the church itself. One gets the impression that the changes are happening mostly around the church, which finds itself 'in the midst of the changes and newness' and so is challenged to respond with a new evangelization. But great renewal by the Spirit is taking place among the people of God at the grass roots: charismatic groups, prayer ministries and basic Christian or ecclesial communities. Moreover, there already exists in the church a significant, even if still relatively small, number of lay men and women theologians and Bible scholars whose presence and contributions the Final Statement might have cited to support its call for the promotion of the laity in 8.3.3.2.

The same applies to the need to recognize women's contributions in the proclamation of the gospel from the grass roots and the existence of outstanding women biblical scholars. Simply to state that 'women *are going to share* an important role in the life of the Church' (8.3.5.6, emphasis mine) is to imply that they are not already doing so. The issue is not that women are not playing an important role in the church, but that their roles are often not recognized or considered important. This observation is made without prejudice to the fact that the church needs to be open to the full participation of women in all aspects of its life, as is called for in the rest of this section of the Final Statement.

Another important but weakly treated section in the Final Statement concerns the socio-political context (6.2). While the document notes awareness of the widening economic gap between the North and South and the rich and the poor, what it proposes as a means of redressing this imbalance 'in this deformed world' (6.2) is rather vague and greatly inadequate: it speaks of the need to 'discover and destroy the idols' and 'dispel the shadows' that prevent human beings from walking in the light of God. The recommendations for this section (8.3.5.4) emphasize in particular preaching the gospel to the poor, writing commentaries that highlight the socio-political issues, joining in movements 'that are in favour of justice, peace and solidarity with the oppressed', and in collaboration with other churches and religious groups 'to urge governments to announce a biblical sabbath, or a jubilee year, before the year 2000' as a way of cancelling the 'foreign debts of the poorest nations of the world'.

But to bring about a truly new creation in the manner envisaged by Revelation and the Isaiah texts, it is not enough to preach the gospel mainly to the poor while the rich continue to operate as though the God-given riches of the world belonged to them and it is for them to decide how much to share with the poor. Moreover, the debt of the so-called rich nations towards the poorer ones whom they have exploited in the past through the slave trade and colonialism and whom they continue to exploit in many open and clandestine ways today needs to be addressed. This other debt which takes the form of cultural, spiritual, economic and ecological exploitation and dehumanization of whole nations and their heritage is far greater than that of billions of dollars or pounds said to be owed by the so-called poor nations to the rich ones.[12] This real 'deformity of the world' requires a radically new solution such as is envisaged in the key biblical texts quoted in the Final Statement. This last observation brings us to the final section of this study.

Concluding remarks

On the whole the Final Statement holds a great challenge for those who wish to engage in the biblical-pastoral ministry today. The document is worth studying carefully along with *The Interpretation of the Bible in the Church* mentioned earlier in this study, as two historical documents on the interpretation of the Bible which are not directly written by the hierarchy. To the comments already made on the different sections of the Final Statement is to be added that the creation of a new heaven and a new earth in both Isaiah (43.19; 65.17) and Revelation (21.5) are the work of God, or of 'the One sitting on the throne' (Rev. 20.11); 21.5) and the Lamb who becomes the pastor. In each case, the establishment of the new heaven and earth or the making of all things new requires the destruction of the current systems. In the case of Deutero- and Trito-Isaiah, there is the establishment of a brand new world political order where God uses the pagan Cyrus as his 'anointed servant'. In Revelation, the complete destruction of the order and reality of this present cosmos, including 'death and Hades' (Rev. 20.14; 21.4).

The new world order that comes into existence is one where the lion can lie down with the lamb, with a little child leading them (cf. Isa. 11.6–9); this is seen as happening in real life, not in a circus. It is one where people of every tribe, language and nation become truly God's people (Rev. 5.9–10); where everyone is accorded his/her dignity and rights as the first born child of God and a citizen of heaven on earth (Heb. 12.22–23); and where no one is regarded as an alien or a stranger. For this to happen, certain categories of people must cease to exist: 'fools', 'idolators' and 'murderers', that is, those who pretend that there is no God (Ps. 14.1), who store up the riches of the world for themselves, and who practise all kinds of falsehood and deceit in their personal, national and international dealings with other human beings and with God.

The biblical-pastoral apostolate is growing and spreading like wildfire. Wildfire here has the quality of the burning bush. People like Moses can go to see and admire the wonders which God is doing (Ex. 3.1–6), but when the time comes for action and commitment to the meaning of the vision and the wonders, we can and often do say like Moses, 'If it please you, my Lord, send someone else' (Ex. 4.13). So the greatest challenge posed by the Final Statement is not simply the multiplication and distribution of Bibles, even though this is also important. The saying of St Jerome that 'ignorance of the Bible is ignorance of Christ' has become a commonplace. But it is also possible to know the scriptures very well and yet not know Christ (John 5.39–39; Matt. 7.21–28). The greatest challenge is on the one hand that of commitment or conversion, allowing the Spirit of God to bring about in one's heart and attitude that 'spiritual revolution' which enables one to become in deed and in truth 'a new creation' (II Cor. 5.17) on the personal, communal, national and global levels; and on the other, that of empowering people to take up their lives and live in a spirit of mutual respect and co-responsibility for common tenantship of the earth.[12]

The first Pentecost resulted in the establishment of a brand new social order among the group of believers (Acts 2.42–47; 4.32–47). It cost them to do so. Jews, for instance, had to learn to call pagans brothers and sisters and eat or share communion fellowship with them, contrary to their previous religious and cultural beliefs and upbringing (Acts 10–11). In our times, it will not be possible to participate in God's activity of 'making all things new' unless we address with all honesty and integrity the issue of racism in all its many subtle forms. For racism is an endemic evil which has undermined and continues to undermine all efforts to proclaim the gospel or to advance the biblical-pastoral apostolate by the Catholic Biblical Federation and the universal church.

When this demon with its legion companions is cast out in all its forms, humanity will gain new eyes and new energy to see and participate in God's project of making all things new. Humanity might then return to that state of unity and solidarity which it had before Babel (Gen. 11.1–9), and which has now been more eminently restored in Christ. Then the biblical-pastoral apostolate of the Catholic Biblical Federation will achieve its goal in proclaiming the Good News that in Christ, God has indeed made all things new here on this our earth, and that believers are living witnesses to it.

Notes

1. The Final Statement of the assembly can be obtained from the General Secretariat of the Catholic Biblical Federation, Mittelstrasse 12, Postfach 10 52 22, D-7000 Stuttgart 10, Germany.

2. The Catholic Biblical Federation came into existence in 1969, four years after the promulgation of the Constitution on Divine Revelation, *Dei Verbum*. It was first founded by the Secretariat for the Promotion of Christian Unity, but gained official status from the Vatican in 1985. Cf. *Bulletin Dei Verbum* 19, 1991, 4.

3. Cf. Ibid., 5.

4. The event is considered as 'providential' because the Catholic Biblical Foundation owes its *raison d'être* to *Dei Verbum*.

5. Here the Final Statement cites the speech of Pope John Paul II to the nineteenth Plenary Assembly of CELAM, Haiti, 9 March 1990.

6. All these points are backed in the Final Statement with scripture references.

7. T. Okure, 'Inculturation: Biblical/Theological Bases', in T. Okure, Paul van Thiel et al., *32 Articles Evaluating the Inculturation of Christianity in Africa*, Eldoret 1990, 56–88, esp. 58.

8. Pontifical Biblical Commission, *The Interpretation of the Bible in the Church*, Rome 1993.

9. Ibid., 18–19.

10. Ibid., section IV, pp. 35–40.

11. See, for instance, *Bulletin Dei Verbum*, nos. 19–22.

12. For further elaboration on this issue, see T. Okure, 'Africa: A Refugee Camp Experience', *Concilium*, 1993/4, 12–21.

The Active Participation of the Church of Zaire in Building a Responsible Nation

For rather more than four years the Republic of Zaire has been working to promote a new type of society, which will help the people to take their destiny into their own hands.

The forward progress of the people of Zaire has cost much sacrifice, and there have been many obstacles in its way. We have to note the flaws in the social project of the Second Republic and the breakdown of a national consensus.

Since the way to be travelled is still long and has many pitfalls, to cover it safely requires a keen sense of responsibility, vigilance and discernment from the people. To strip off the old man and discover in everyone a brother or sister created in the image of God constitutes a profession of faith intent on improving the present situation and building a constitutional state which will be peaceful and prosperous, once the agreement of men and women of good will has been secured.

So since the process of democratization was launched in 1990, by popular demand, the church of Zaire has not ceased to follow the course that has been embarked on and to call on the nation to mobilize and show its commitment to the creation of a constitutional state, despite the problems of the process.

Furthermore, in order to remedy a killing ignorance, in this development the church has sought to remind the people of their role as the main subject and agent of democratization. And its commitment to the service of the people and of peace remains constant, above all in difficult times, the most critical of these being the period, happily now over, of the division of national institutions.

The signing of a protocol of agreement in which all accepted a single constitution has allowed a clear definition of the rules of democracy, serving as a reference point in all situations for politicians from now on, even if it is still not always observed.

This advance makes it possible for all to join responsibly in the project of achieving a common national society, which was described so well by Pope John Paul II in *Christifideles laici* (no. 15): 'The lay faithful cannot renounce participation in politics, the many forms of economic, social, legislative, administrative, cultural action aimed at promoting the common good, organically and through institutions.'

The need to hold elections

The church notes that this progress along the way of democratization calls for elections, and these in turn require certain basic conditions if they are to be held. A reasonable period needs to be allowed for the campaign and the electoral process to be prepared carefully and not rushed, so that people and property are safe and radio and television are liberalized. Channels of communication need to be reopened, and the national community needs a restoration of the essential means through which the state can function: the territorial army, national security, a central bank, para-state organizations, the office of customs and excises, the tax office.

It is equally important to purge the social and political climate, all the more since some politicians opposed to elections are doing everything possible to prevent them taking place in good conditions.

Hence the tendency towards ethnicization and regionalization in politics. This so-called 'geopolitical' policy of division is leading to the destruction of the country and the negation of the nation of Zaire. To see how this is happening, one need only recall the political exploitation of certain tribal antagonisms which led to bloodshed and destruction, particularly in the regions of Shaba and North Kivu.

It is quite evident that if the elections take place in such a context, the resultant chaos may well land the country in the same situation as prevailed in the Congo in the 1960s.

To avoid an apocalypse of which there is a considerable risk because of the existence of militant partisans, the church emphasizes the need to train the people of Zaire to see why it is so important to create a nation. This means leading people and groups of different metalities to become and really to form a nation, a common heritage for which citizens can demand and defend, with assurance and determination, a democratic system of government.

Does democracy only exist where a nation is aware of defending something that it possesses? In this perspective the church, which is not involved in politics in its own interest and affirms that in Zaire no one must engage in politics in his own name and on his own account, is giving itself the role, through its hierarchy, of helping lay Christians to fulfil their mission faithfully and to renew the temporal in a way which conforms to the demands of the gospel.

However, certain questions deserve its special attention in the task of educating the population, notably the national character of Zairean politics, the rights and duties of citizens, a sense of the common good and vigilance against violence and corruption.

In this context the church can arouse the conscience of the people to a common cause dictated by common problems: health, food, teaching, and development of the riches offered by nature in conformity with justice.

The church can equally help to promote a sense of solidarity and cement national unity by protecting the population against the speeches and practices of those who preach division and demobilization.

The process of democratization above all, for the church too, bears with it the responsibility for everyone to engage in politics in order to defend and maintain a common heritage, respect for the public good, the productive work with a view towards increasing the national heritage, to be done with a view to the benefit of the whole community.

In politics the church encourages a constructive, courteous, educative and honest competition, purged of all desire for hegemony and the exclusion of any group, tribe or nation, and the prevention of any actions which are injurious, defamatory or crude. In short, politics is a place of sanctification for Christians.

A profile for leaders

Since the crisis involving all the people of Zaire is above all that of politicians, the church invites these politicians to rid themselves of every vice and become models for society, abounding in moral and civic virtues, pledges of a society which organizes an alternation of power, in which economic investment contracts concluded by the leaders aim at the interest of the nation, the common good, and in which the leaders take responsibility for their successes and failures, without seeking scapegoats.

Congratulating the people on its capacity to endure and resist the temptations of despair and violence, the church exhorts them to look carefully at the profiles of future political leaders during the next elections. In their message 'Stand Firm in the Faith' (no. 8), addressed to the Catholic faithful, the bishops of Zaire wrote: 'If we are going to emerge from the present crisis and make progress, let us entrust the government of the country to those among us whose honesty, competence, experience, love of peace, concern for national unity, seriousness and devotion to public and private affairs are solidly established.'

In the same document priests, religious and pastoral workers were invited to preserve peace and concord based on justice among all men and women and not to take an active part in political parties and the activity of trade unions except to defend the rights of the church or to promote the common good, first having consulted the hierarchy.

The church of Zaire distinguishes its roles and competences from those of the state and bars the clergy from any active role in the conduct of the affairs of state.

The contribution of the church towards the training of the people is aimed essentially at letting them be responsible for everyday life, for becoming a nation, fighting division and the tribalization of social and political problems, and engaging in the development projects which have begun, with a view to improving the environment, food and housing and educating young people and adults in public health.

The church is also involved in helping the people to understand what democracy is about, with a view towards their making a judicious choice of the administrations that are needed by neighbourhoods, villages, groups, zones, regions and the country as a whole so that it can progress and enjoy cultural, social, economic, political and moral development.

A people which is well trained, well informed and well educated is more capable of taking on the various tasks which conscience dictates in defence of a common heritage, whatever the sacrifice, without allowing itself to be submerged by a spirit of destruction, hatred and division.

Finally, the church asks partners outside Zaire to pay close attention not to the service expected by a personality or group of persons but the advantage offered by co-operation to the whole of the national community. It also asks that there should be no encouragement of division or violence, but that work should be done for peace and the consolidation of democratic institutions in the country, leading to more solid and stable international relations.

The Catholic church constantly invites its members to resort to spiritual means so that God, who is the sole master of humankind and history, will accomplish the good that he has begun for the people of Zaire. These means are, in particular, constant prayer, renunciation, penitence and disinterested work for the good of all.

Emery Kabongo Kanundowi, Archbishop of Luebo
and Vice-President of the Episcopal Conference of Zaire

The editors of the Special Column are Norbert Greinacher and Bas van Iersel. The content of the Special Column does not necessarily reflect the views of the Editorial Board of Concilium.

Contributors

OTHMAR KEEL was born in Einsiedeln, Switzerland, in 1937 and studied theology, religion and the Bible, the history of ancient Near Eastern art and Egyptian in Zurich, Fribourg, Rome, Jerusalem and Chicago. Since 1969 he has been Professor in the Theological Faculty of the University of Fribourg, Switzerland. His special area is the relationships between the linguistic imagery of the Old Testament and ancient Near Eastern pictorial art, especially that of the seal amulets. He is founder and editor of the series Orbis Biblicus et Orientalis, in which 138 volumes have been published since 1937. He has written 22 books and around 100 articles. The most important books are: *The Symbolism of the Biblical World. Ancient Near Eastern Iconography and the Book of Psalms*, New York 1978; *Jahwes Entgegnung an Ijob*, Göttingen 1978; *The Song of Songs*, New York 1994; (with M. Küchler) *Orte und Landschaften der Bibel. Ein Handbuch und Studienreiseführer zum heiligen Land* (2 vols), Zurich and Göttingen 1982, 1984; (with H. Keel-Leu, S. Schroer et al.), *Studien zu Stempelsiegeln aus Palästina/Israel* (4 vols), Fribourg and Göttingen 1985–94; (with C. Uehlinger), *Göttinen, Götter und Gottessymbole. Neue Erkenntnisse zur Religionsgeschichte Kanaans und Israel aufgrund bislang unerschlossener ikonographischer Quellen*, Quaestiones disputate 134, Freiburg in Breisgau ²1993.

Address: Biblische Institut, Universität Misericorde, CH 1700 Fribourg, Switzerland.

JACQUES VAN RUITEN was born in 1956. He studied theology and Judaica in London and Amsterdam, and gained his doctorate in 1984 and his promotion in 1990 in the Catholic Theological University of Amsterdam in 1990. He is a university lecturer in Israelite literature, Old Testament exegesis and early Jewish literature at the Rijksuniversiteit Groningen. He is a member of the editorial board of the *Journal for the Study of Judaism in the Persian, Hellenistic and Roman Period*. He has written *Een begin zonder einde. De doorwerking van Jesaja 65:17 in de intertestamentaire literatuur en het Nieuwe Testament*, Sliedrecht 1990, and articles in the sphere of the Old Testament and the history of the reception of Old Testament texts in early Jewish literature.

Address: Middelhorsterweg 47, 9751 TB Haren, Netherlands.

WILLARD G. OXTOBY has been professor in the comparative study of religion at the University of Toronto since 1971, and formerly taught at McGill University (Montreal) and at Yale University. He has been president of the American Society for the Study of Religion and co-president of the 33rd International Congress of Asian and North African Studies. His short book *The Meaning of Other Faiths*, Philadelphia 1983, is also published in German as *Offenes Christentum*, Munich 1986, and in Chinese as *Chi-tu chiao yu ch'i-t'a tsung-chiao*, Tainan 1985. He is currently editing a two-volume introduction to the world's great religions, in which he has contributed a major section on Christianity. He also deals with Middle Eastern religion before Islam, and questions of method and theory in the study of religion.

Address: Trinity College, University of Toronto, Toronto M5S 18H, Canada.

JOHN RICHES is Professor of Divinity and Biblical Criticism at the University of Glasgow. Born in 1939, he studied in Cambridge, Bethel and Göttingen, was ordained priest in 1966 and worked in Norfolk and Cambridge before moving in 1972 to Glasgow to teach New Testament. He has combined this with work in a parish in downtown Glasgow, involvement in a small development trust and teaching in Transkei, South Africa. He is at present working with the Catholic Institute of West Africa on research into the relationship between popular and academic readings of the Bible. As well as producing studies of first-century Judaism and the history of New Testament scholarship, he edited the translation of von Balthasar's *The Glory of the Lord*. He is planning a history of the interpretation of Galatians. Publications: *Jesus and the Transformation of Judaism*, London 1980; *The World of Jesus*, Cambridge 1990; *A Century of New Testament Studies*, Cambridge 1993.

Address: The University of Glasgow, Department of Biblical Studies, Glasgow G12 8QQ, Scotland.

DAVID JASPER is Reader in Literature and Theology and Director of the Centre for the Study of Literature and Theology, University of Glasgow. He is also an Anglican priest. He was previously Principal of St Chad's

College, University of Durham. He holds degrees in English literature from Cambridge, and theology from Oxford. His doctoral work at the University of Durham was on S. T. Coleridge. He is editor of the journal *Literature and Theology*, and general editor of the series *Studies in Literature and Religion*. He is the author of numerous articles and books; his most recent book is *Rhetoric, Power and Community* (1993). Dr Jasper has lectured in the USA, Australia, Israel and widely in Europe, and has organized a series of international conferences on literature and theology in both Durham and Glasgow.

Address: Centre for the Study of Literature and Theology, Department of English Literature, University of Glasgow, Glasgow G12 8QQ, Scotland.

ARNULF CAMPS was born in Eindhoven, The Netherlands, in 1925. He joined the Franciscans in 1943 and was ordained priest in 1950. He studied missiology at the University of Fribourg, Switzerland, and gained his doctorate in theology in 1957 with a dissertation on Jerome Xavier SJ and the Muslims of the Mogul Empire. From 1957 to 1961 he was professor at the regional major seminary of Christ the King in Karachi, Pakistan; from 1961 to 1963 mission secretary of the Dutch Franciscans and from 1963 to 1990 professor of missiology at the Catholic University of Nijmegen. From 1964 to 1980 he was *consultor* to the Papal Council for Inter-religious Dialogue in Rome, and from 1967 a member of the governing body of the inter-university Institute for Missiology and Ecumenics at Utrecht and Leiden, from 1981 to 1991 being its president. He helped to found the International Association for Mission Studies in 1968 and was its president for four years. His publications include: *Christendom en godsdiensten der wereld*, Baarn 1976; *De weg, de paden en de wegen*, Baarn 1977; *Geen doodlopende weg*, Baarn 1978; *Partners in Dialogue*, New York 1983; *The Sanskrit Grammar and Manuscripts of Father Heinrich Roth SJ*, Leiden 1988; *Het derde oog*, Nijmegen 1990.

Address: Helmkruidstraat 35, 6602 CZ Wychen, Netherlands.

JEAN-PIERRE RUIZ was ordained a priest of the diocese of Brooklyn, New York, in 1982, after theological training at the Gregorian University in Rome where in 1989 he earned the STD. He has served as Professor of Biblical Studies at Pope John XXIII National Seminary in Weston, Massachusetts. He now teaches biblical studies at St John's University in New York. He is a member of the Catholic Biblical Association of America, the Society of Biblical Literature and the Academy of Catholic Hispanic Theologians of the United States. His publications include

Ezekiel in the Apocalypse: The Transformation of Prophetic Language in Revelation 16.17–19.10, Frankfurt 1989, and 'Beginning to Read the Bible in Spanish: An Initial Assessment', *Journal of Hispanic/Latino Theology* 1.2, February 1994, 28–50.

Address: St John's University, 8000 Utopia Parkway, Jamaica, New York 11439, USA.

GEORGE M. SOARES-PRABHU, an Indian Jesuit, has been teaching New Testament at Jnana Deepa Vidyapeeth, the Pontifical Athenaeum at Pune, India, since 1969. His publications include *The Formula Quotations in the Infancy Narrative of Matthew*, Rome 1976; *Wir werden bei ihm wohnen: Das Johannesevangelium in indischer Deutung*, Freiburg 1984; *Inculturation, Liberation, Dialogue: Challenges to Christian Theology in Asia Today*, Pune 1984, and several articles in biblical and missiological journals.

Address: De Nobili College, Pune 411014, India.

NORMAN SOLOMON was born in Cardiff, South Wales, and educated at Cardiff High School and St John's College, Cambridge. As an Orthodox rabbi, he has ministered to congregations in Manchester, Liverpool, London and Birmingham. He is Founder Director of the Centre for the Study of Judaism and Jewish/Christian Relations at the Selly Oak Colleges, Birmingham, Recognized Lecturer of the Department of Theology, University of Birmingham, and Visiting Lecturer to the Oxford Centre for Postgraduate Hebrew Studies. He has published two full-length books: *Judaism and World Religion*, London and New York 1991, and *The Analytic Movement: Hayyim Soloveitchik and his School*, Atlanta 1993. From 1985–9 he edited the quarterly *Christian-Jewish Relations* for the Institute of Jewish Affairs. He is an Adviser to the International Council of Christians and Jews, and a regular participant in major international Jewish/Christian consultations.

Address: 50 Estria Road, Edgbaston, Birmingham B15 2LQ.

TERESA OKURE, SHJC is a Nigerian. She is Academic Dean of the Catholic Higher Theological Institute of West Africa (CIWA), Nigeria, and a professor in Sacred Scripture. Formerly the Executive Secretary of EATWOT, she currently serves on the Advisory Committee of *Concilium* for Moral Theology and the Executive Committee of the International Association for Mission Studies and the EATWOT Commission for the

Study of Theology. Her books include *The Johannine Approach to Mission: A Contextual Study of John 4:1–42*, Tübingen *1988*, and *32 Articles Evaluating the Inculturation of Christianity in Africa*, Gaba 1990, of which she is co-author, and her articles include 'Leadership in the New Testament', *Nigerian Journal of Theology* 1.5, 1990, 72–93, and 'The Significance Today of Jesus' Commission to Mary Magdalene', *International Review of Mission* LXXXI.322, 1992.

Address: Catholic Institute of West Africa, PO Box 499, Port Harcourt, Nigeria.

Members of the Advisory Committee for Exegesis